D0468422
STEADY BEAT

Steady Beat Vol. 1

Created by Rivkah

Lettering and Graphic Designer - Gloria Wu
Cover Design - Gary Shum

Editor - Rob Valois
Digital Imaging Manager - Chris Buford
Production Managers - Jennifer Miller and Mutsumi Miyazaki
Managing Editor - Lindsey Johnston
Editorial Director - Jeremy Ross
VP of Production - Ron Klamert
Publisher and E.I.C. - Mike Kiley
President and C.O.O. - John Parker
C.E.O. - Stuart Levy

A TOKYOPOP® Manga

TOKYOPOP Inc.
5900 Wilshire Blvd. Suite 2000
Los Angeles, CA 90036

E-mail: info@TOKYOPOP.com
Come visit us online at www.TOKYOPOP.com

ISBN: 1-59816-135-0

First TOKYOPOP printing: October 2005

10 9 8 7 6 5 4 3 2 1

Printed in the USA

TOKYOPOP®
PRESENTS
Steady Beat™

BEAT 1

EASTLAKE 15th
ANNUAL SOCCER CHAMPIONSHIP
Stay Calm.

Focus.
RUSH
I'm not going to lose!
THWOCK

GO!!!
GO!!!
GO!!!
...WHO IS SHE?
THAT GIRL POPPED OUT OF NOWHERE...

LEAH WINTERS SCORES!!!
#13
EAST-LAK TAKES T LEAD!
LEAH!
OVER HERE!
JUNE,
I DIDN'T THINK YOU WERE GOING TO BE ABLE TO MAKE IT.
I TOLD MOM I WAS HEADED TO THE LIBRARY TO WORK ON OUR ENGLISH REPORT...
...SHE ACTUALLY BELIEVED ME THIS TIME.

Leah Winters:
Age: 16
Birthday: November 1st
Sign: Scorpio
Eye Color: Hazel
Height: 5'7"

Likes: Chinese Food, TexMex, and Chocolate. The colors green and yellow. Math & Science classes. Reading textbooks "for fun." Beating up boys.

Dislikes: Country music. Japanese food (not enough spice!). English class. The color pink. Politics. Religion.

perfect
YOU WERE AWESOME OUT THERE!
SARAI COULDN'T HAVE DONE BETTER!
TWEEEEEEEEEEEEEET
UGH!
WHY DID YOU HAVE TO MENTION MY SISTER?
*GROAN
#13
SHOVE
LEAH!
WHAT ARE YOU ALL EXCITED ABOUT?
Not so perfect

NOW GET BACK INTO POSITION BEFORE I KICK YOUR SKINNY BUTT!
I TOLD YOU TO DEFEND THE BACK! NOT TAKE THE FRONT!!
HI, SARAI...
...I DIDN'T KNOW YOU WERE COACHING TODAY.
SHE WASN'T SUPPOSED TO...BUT COACH IS OUT SICK.
It only makes sense for the captain of the varsity team to take over.
HOW ARE YOU MY SISTER AGAIN?
YOU SHOUL BE HAPPY SCORE

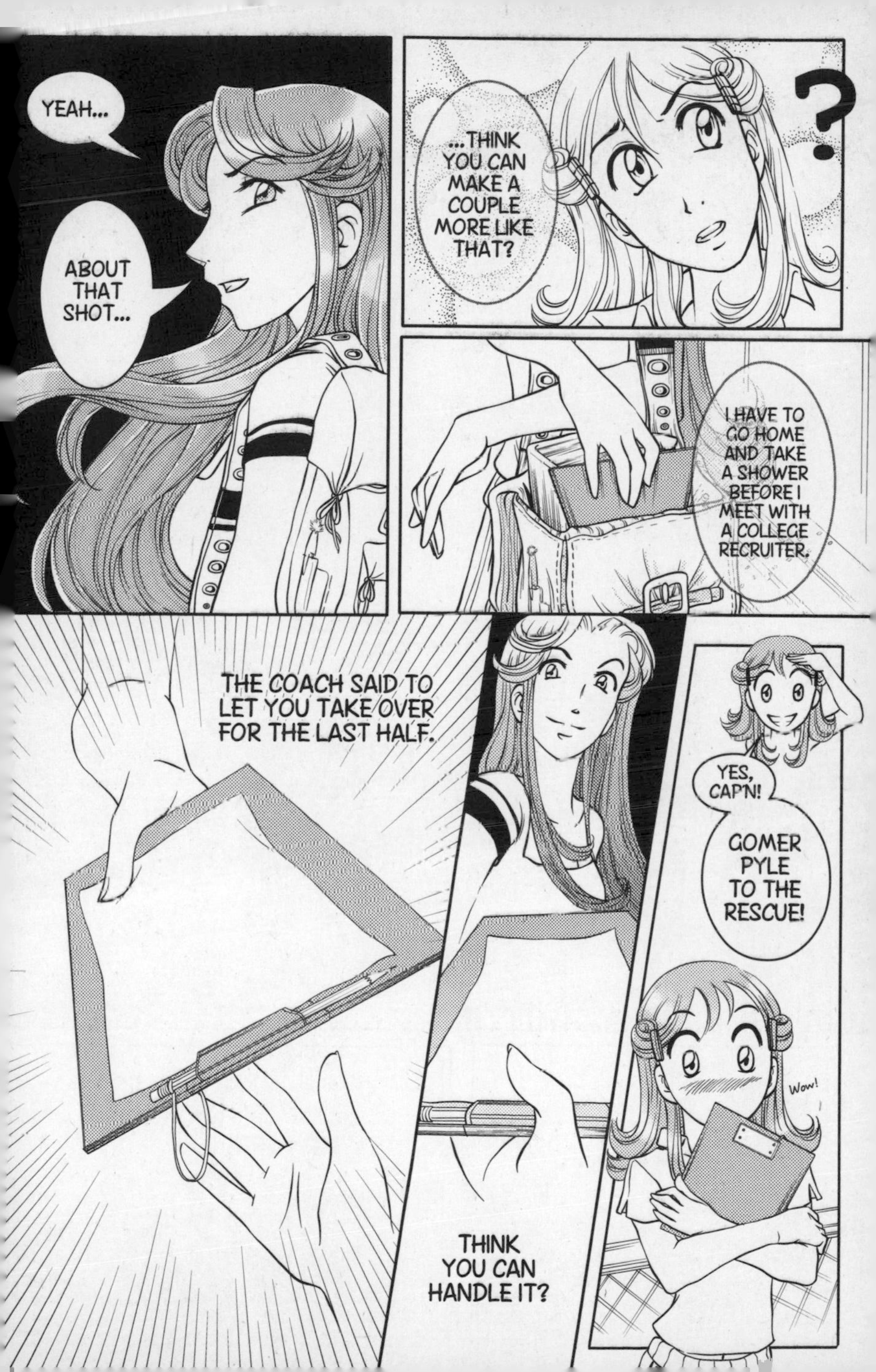
YEAH...
ABOUT THAT SHOT...
...THINK YOU CAN MAKE A COUPLE MORE LIKE THAT?
?
I HAVE TO GO HOME AND TAKE A SHOWER BEFORE I MEET WITH A COLLEGE RECRUITER.
THE COACH SAID TO LET YOU TAKE OVER FOR THE LAST HALF.
THINK YOU CAN HANDLE IT?
YES, CAP'N!
GOMER PYLE TO THE RESCUE!
Wow!

AND DON'T FORGET...
...DEFENSE!
NO WAY!
ALL RIGHT!!!
I'M GOING TO PROVE I'M A BETTER COACH THAN SHE IS!!!
LET'S GO!!!
CRACKLE
CRACKLE

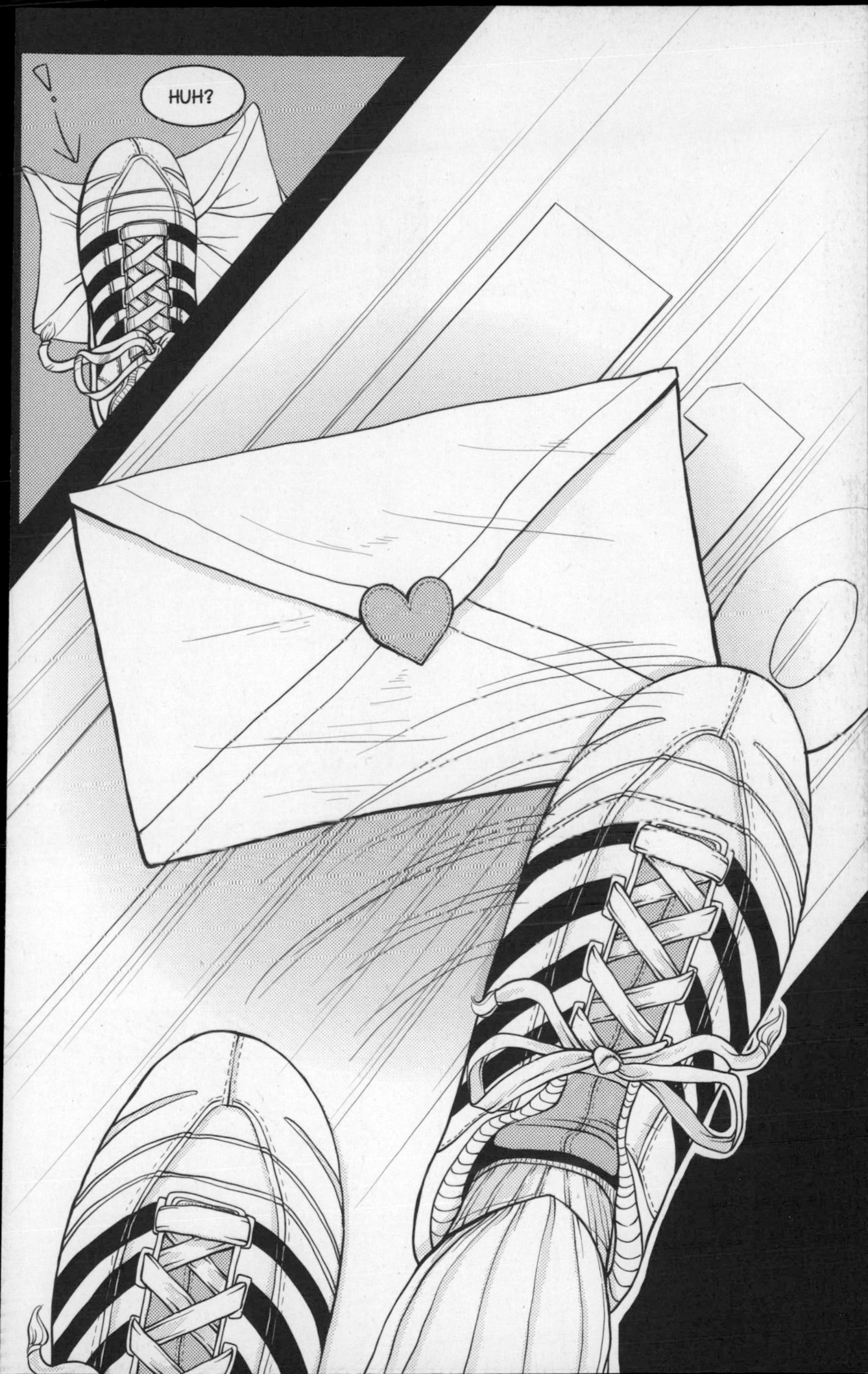
HUH?

SHOULDN'T YOU BE GETTING BACK TO THE GAME?
YEAH, IN A MINUTE.
WHAT'S THAT?

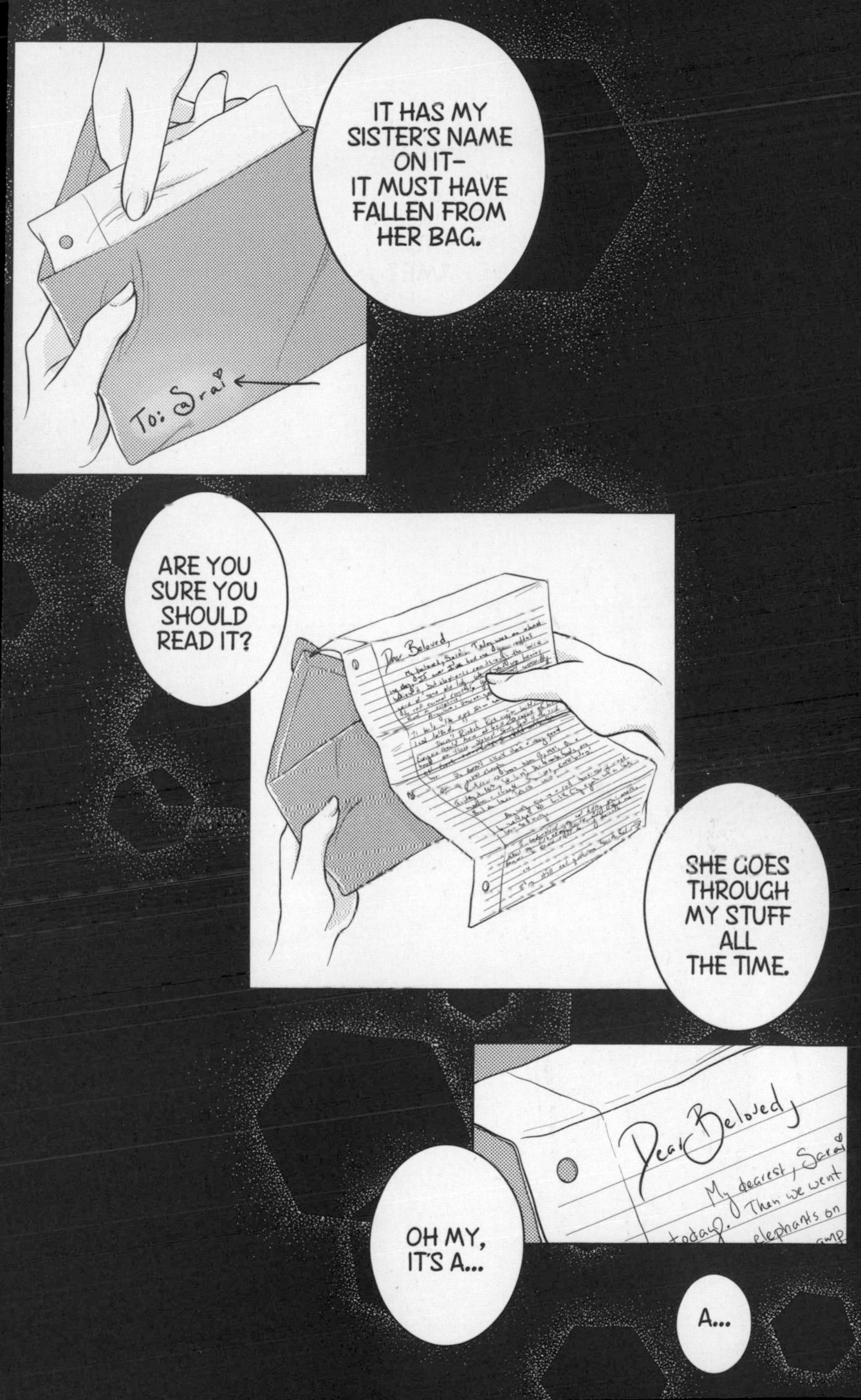
IT HAS MY SISTER'S NAME ON IT— IT MUST HAVE FALLEN FROM HER BAG.
To: Sarai
ARE YOU SURE YOU SHOULD READ IT?
Dear Beloved,
SHE GOES THROUGH MY STUFF ALL THE TIME.
Dear Beloved,
My dearest, Sarai
Then we went
today.
elephants on
OH MY, IT'S A...
A...

...A LOVE LETTER!
LET ME SEE!!!
Why is everybody knocking me around?
EWW!
THIS IS SO CHEESY!

LISTEN TO THIS!
"MY BELOVED SARAI, I'M SORRY ABOUT OUR FIGHT THE OTHER DAY..."
"I KNOW I WAS WRONG TO ASK YOU WHAT I DID."
WHOA!
A LOVERS' QUARREL.
"FORGIVE ME?"
HUH?
THAT'S ODD...
THERE'S MORE OF THE UNUSUSAL MUSHY STUFF:
"YOUR EYES ARE LIKE SAPPHIRES" YADA YADA
AND THEN:
"OUR LOVE IS ETERNAL" YADA YADA
"I'M SORRY ABOUT YOUR MOTHER THE OTHER DAY, TOO. REALLY SORRY. BUT I DON'T THINK SHE SAW US."
"LET ME MAKE IT UP TO YOU."
"I'LL BE WAITING AT OUR USUAL SPOT."
"MEET ME AT 5."
"DON'T BE LATE!"
"LOVE--"

Love, Jessica
Go!
Go!
Go!
Go!
THAT CHANGES THE DYNAMIC A BIT.
"JESSICA" AIN'T EXACTLY A BOY'S NAME.
GRAB
ARE WE SURE THIS IS TO MY SISTER?
Wooooo

Bzzzzt!!!!!!!
¡Go Team!
YO, LEAH!
GET YOUR BUTT OVER HERE!
THE GAME IS ABOUT TO START BACK UP!
LEAH...
...WORRY ABOUT THIS LATER, OKAY?

Ha
Ha
Ha
CLICK
C'MON GIRL!
FOCUS!
CLICK
YOU'RE THE COACH NOW.
CLICK

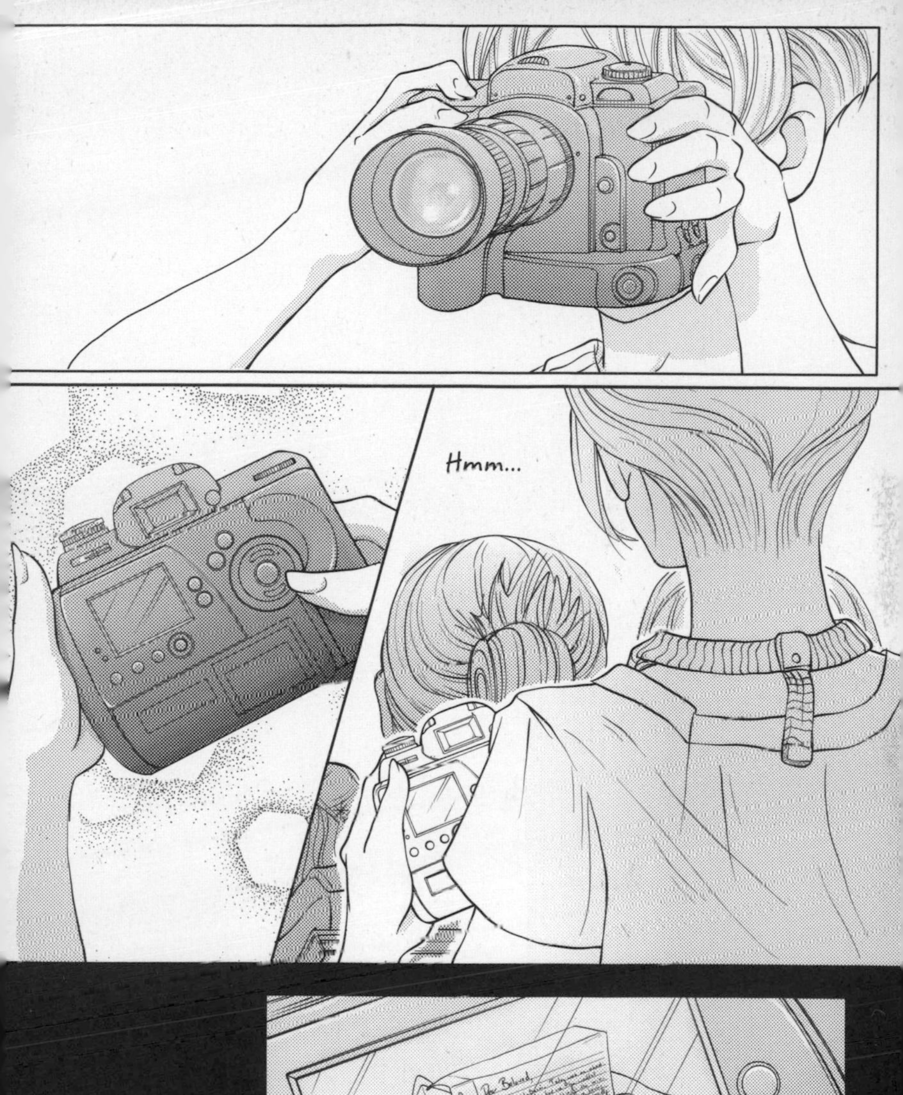
Hmm...

...a letter.

WHOO-HOO!
GO TEAM!
SOS
SOS

Interesting.
I wonder what's in that letter...
...and why our class valedictorian and star soccer player is leaving in the middle of the game.

Is there a story behind this?

BEAT 1 END

BEAT 2

4424
WINTERS
When I saw that letter--
When I saw that name--
I'M HOME!
My heart nearly stopped.

I couldn't concentrate on the game.
EHS
I couldn't focus on the goal.
All I could think about was asking my sister about that girl.
A girl named Jessica!
How do you ask something like that?
"Hey sis..."
"...are you gay?"

She'd kill me!
And Sarai's brought boyfriends home before.
I know she's been on dates with them.
Who knows what else she's done!!!
She is 18!
I could be wrong.

WHAT ARE YOU STARING AT?
YOU LOOK GUILTY.
YOU LOST THE GAME, DIDN'T YOU?
ONLY BY A COUPLE OF POINTS.
IT'S NO BIG DEAL.
HMM...
NO WONDE YOU LOST.
I MEAN, SERIOUSLY...
...YOU'LL NEVER GET ANYWHERE IF YOU ACCEPT FAILURE.

silence
WHAT ARE THOSE?

HMN?
THESE?
THEY'RE FLOWERS, DUFUS.
CRINKLE
IT'S A GOOD LUCK GIFT,
BUT...
...THEY'RE JUST FROM A FRIEND.

"Just" a friend?
Is this like the girl who's "just" a roommate...
...but there's only one bedroom?
What kind of "friend" sends red roses?
IT'S JUST LIKE IN THOSE OLD ROMANCE COMICS:
OUR HEROINE FINDS HERSELF AT THE CLIFF OF SUDDEN EPIPHANY. SHE MUST MAKE A DECISION.
DOES SHE EXPOSE THIS DARK SECRET AND RUIN THE LIFE OF SOMEONE SHE CARES ABOUT...
...OR DOES SHE PROTECT THIS SECRET?
HER CHOICE IS CLEAR:

SHE'LL KILL SARAI!
MOM CAN'T FIND OUT!!!
And then it would be...
...just me...
...and mom.
I CAN'T LET THAT HAPPEN!!!
MOM ONLY LETS ME ALONE BECAUSE SHE HAS SARAI TO FUSS OVER!
THAT MAD-WOMAN WOULD GIVE ME A HEART ATTACK BY THE TIME I'M 20!

HEY, WEIRDO.
WHAT'S WITH THE SILENT HYSTERICS?
← Big Sister Glow
I DIDN'T MEAN TO UPSET YOU.
I'M SURE THE NEXT GAME WILL BE FINE.
Little Sister Confusion: not used to Big-Sis being nice)
BUT...
...YOU KNOW...
!
RIVKAH/LEAH INSTANT MESSAGING DIALOG:
LEAH: WHY CAN'T PEOPLE READ MINDS AND GET THIS PART OVER WITH?! THIS IS SO EMBARRASSING.
RIVKAH: BECAUSE THEN I'D HAVE NO STORY AND WOULD BE JUST ANOTHER STARVING ARTIST & WRITER.
LEAH: YOU *ARE* A STARVING ARTIST . . . BUT YOU *COULD* HAVE MADE ME A MAGICAL GIRL INSTEAD . . .
RIVKAH: SAY THAT AGAIN, AND YOU'LL BE WEARING A CAPE AND TIGHTS!

...YOU WOULD HAVE WON IF YOU'D ACTUALLY LISTENED TO ME!
I SAID DEFENSE!
DEFENSE!
CAN'T YOU JUST LEAVE ME ALONE?
WHATEVER.
I CAN TELL WHEN YOU'RE UPSET, SIGHING AND STOMPING AROUND.
KINDA LIKE A TWO YEAR OLD.
DON'T WORRY.
YOU'LL GROW OUT OF IT.
BUT I GOTTA GO.
I'LL SHOW YOU HOW TO COACH THE RIGHT WAY, TOMORROW!
SLAM
WHAT THE HECK WAS THAT SUPPOSED TO MEAN?!
WE LOST BECAUSE OF HER STUPID LETTER!
This is Leah lyi
to herself.

And it's not like I even care about the game anyway.
I'm worried for her life!
So precious!
Only to have it taken away at the hands of our own mother!
...Why can't I just ask her?
I think I'm gonna be sick...

I think a part of me has...
...always known
brring
brring
brring

WINTERS' RESIDENCE.
HELLO?
CRASH
CLATTER
CLATTER
THUNK
Silence

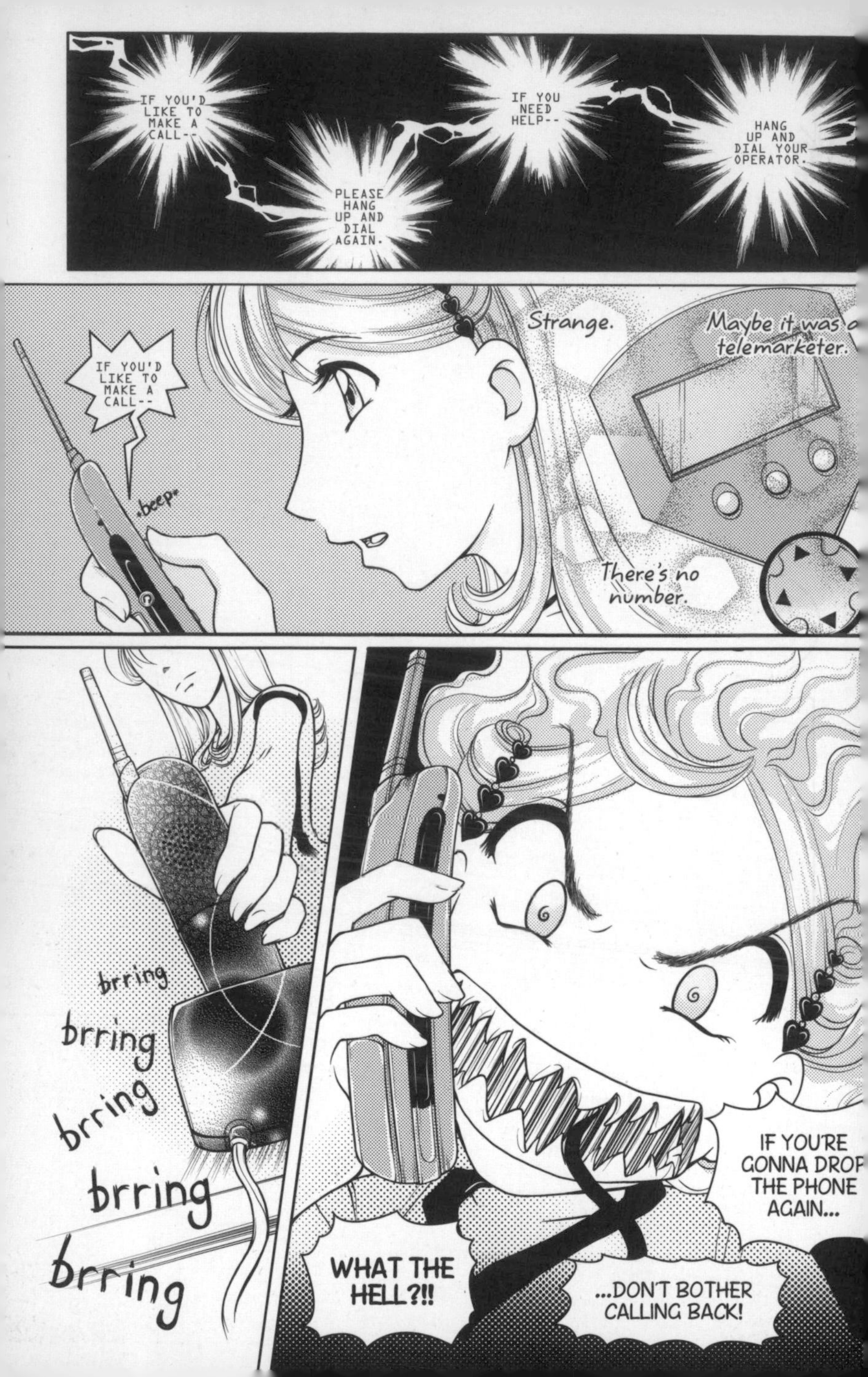
IF YOU'D LIKE TO MAKE A CALL--
PLEASE HANG UP AND DIAL AGAIN.
IF YOU NEED HELP--
HANG UP AND DIAL YOUR OPERATOR.
IF YOU'D LIKE TO MAKE A CALL--
beep
Strange.
There's no number.
Maybe it was a telemarketer.
brring
brring
brring
brring
brring
WHAT THE HELL?!!
IF YOU'RE GONNA DROP THE PHONE AGAIN...
...DON'T BOTHER CALLING BACK!

HAVING ISSUES, SWEETIE?
IT'S ME.
MOM.
I'M CALLIN' TO CHECK UP ON YOU.
AND YOU SHOULDN'T SAY "HELL."
"HELL" ISN'T A SWEAR WORD...
YES IT IS!
NO IT'S NOT.
IF YOU'RE LOOKING FOR SARAI, SHE LEFT ALREADY.
SHE'S SUCH A GOOD GIRL!
I HOPE SHE DIDN'T FORGET TO TAKE HER TEST SCORES...
DOES SARAI EVER FORGET ANYTHING?
OF COURSE NOT!
How silly of me to think otherwise!

BY THE WAY...
I'M GOING TO BE HOME LATE TONIGHT.
THE REST OF THE STATE SENATORS WANT TO GET TOGETHER BEFORE THE SPRING SESSION BEGINS.
THERE'S SOME PRETTY IMPORTANT LEGISLATION COMING UP.
DON'T DO ANYTHING RASH WHILE I'M OUT, LEAH.
LIKE BURNING DOWN THE HOUSE...
...AGAIN.
MOM!!!
THAT WAS OVER TEN YEARS AGO!
LOOK MOMMY!
I LEARNED HO TO MAKE A VOLCANO AT SCHOOL!
BUT I FOUND THIS MODIFIED RECIPE ON THE INTERNET!
Anarchy
3rd grade Family Portrait
Wee!
MOMMY
ME!
MY HOUSE
BOOM!
MY FAMILY!
I WOULDN'T DO ANYTHING LIKE THAT NOW.

I'D THROW A PARTY, INSTEAD!
YOUNG LADY!!!
DO THAT AND YOU'RE GROUNDED!
FOR LIFE!
OH!
GOTTA GO, MOM!
THE KEG'S HERE!
I WOULDN'T WANT TO EMBARRASS YOU BY BEING IMPOLITE NOW, WOULD I?

BEEP
TALK
LOUD/ SEARCH
HOLD
CLEAR
HMM...
CLICK!
LIKE I'D EVER DO ANYTHING LIKE THAT!
brring
brring
brring
I WAS JUST KIDDING ABOUT THE PARTY!
AND THE KEG!
PLEASE DON'T GROUND ME!!!

WHOA, GIRL!
I PROMISE I WON'T GROUND YOU!
NO...
DID SOMETHING HAPPEN WHEN YOU GOT HOME?
ACTUALLY...
...I WAS JUST HAVING PROBLEMS WITH MY MOM AGAIN.
I WISH SHE'D RELAX A BIT.

BUT SHE'S TOO WRAPPED UP WITH SARAI GETTING INTO A GOOD COLLEGE.
SHE GAVE UP ON ME A LONG TIME AGO.
WHAT'S THAT SUPPOSED TO MEAN?!
WASN'T SHE A DROP-OUT?
AND PREGNANT?!

ANYWAY, YOU'RE ALWAYS GETTING AWESOME TEST SCORES.
WHY SHOULD SHE WORRY?
BUT I HATE DOING HOMEWORK, SO I ONLY PASS BECAUSE OF TESTS AND QUIZZES.
GUESS I'M JUST NATURALLY BRILLIANT.
*AND SHE READS THE TEXTBOOKS... FOR FUN.
OH...
I SEE.
I think I hate you.
HEY!!! WANNA COME OVER AND PLAY?!
I ALREADY READ ALL THE CARDS THOUGH...
I CALLED TO ASK YOU ABOUT OUR ENGLISH HOMEWORK!
NO!
OH...
I SEE.
DON'T WORRY ABOUT IT, LEAH.
WE'LL DO SOMETHING TOMORROW, OKAY?

SNAP
beep
I wish June could come over.
She'd know what to do about Sarai.
Nobody else would understand.
brring
brring
brring

HAT?!
CAN'T A GIRL THINK AROUND HERE?!
I JUST WANT TO ANGST AND FEEL SORRY FOR MYSELF!
BAM
HELLLLLLLLLLLLLLLLLLLLO?
SILENCE

THANK YOU FOR CALLING THE *"PIZZA! PIZZA! LOTTERY!" HELP DESK!
IN ORDER TO CLAIM YOUR PRIZE, PLEASE LEAVE YOUR CREDIT CARD NUMBER, NAME AND SOCIAL SECURITY NUMBER AT THE TONE, AND YOUR BANK WILL NOTIFY YOU IN A FEW DAYS.
*"PIZZA! PIZZA! LOTTERY!" IS A SUBSIDIARY OF THE NICARAGUA BANK TRANSFER FUND. PLEASE USE THE LEAST DISCRETION POSSIBLE WHEN PLACING AN ORDER ONLINE!
CONTINUED SILENCE
FINE THEN!
BE THAT WAY!
I'M HANGING UP AND NOT ANSWERING ANYMORE!
NOBODY EVER WINS THE LOTTERY ANYWAY!

WAIT!
LEAH!

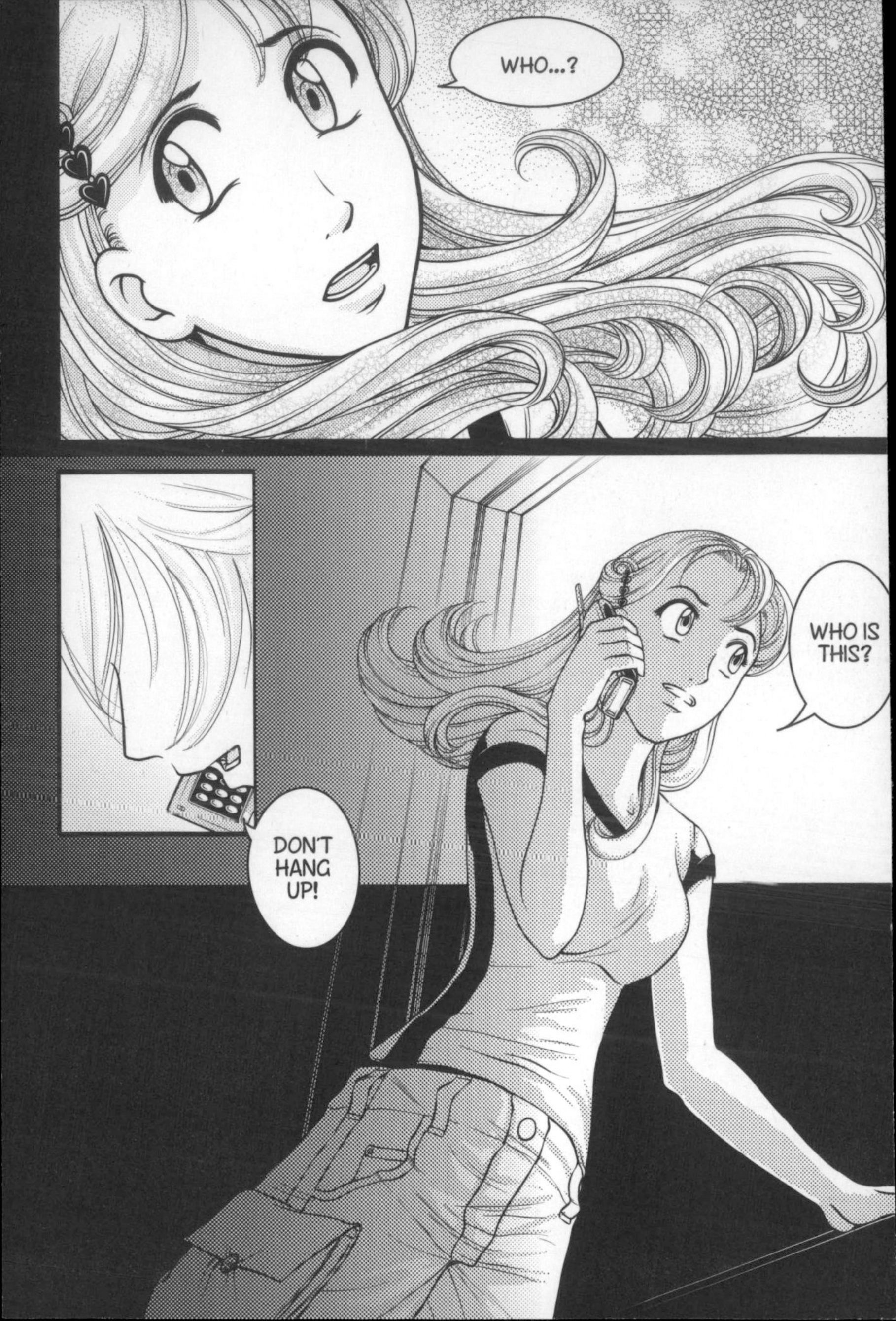
WHO...?
WHO IS THIS?
DON'T HANG UP!

IT'S ABOUT THE LETTER YOU FOUND TODAY...
I KNOW WHAT'S IN IT.

MEET ME AT THE ENTRANCE TO ZILKER PARK IN AN HOUR.
I HAVE SOMETHING TO ASK YOU.
DON'T BE LATE...

BEAT 2 END

BEAT 3

ZILKER PARK
"Meet me at Zilker Park in an hour..."
ZILKER PARK
8:00 AM - 10:00 PM
$2.00 parking
"...Don't be late."

This day just keeps getting better and better.

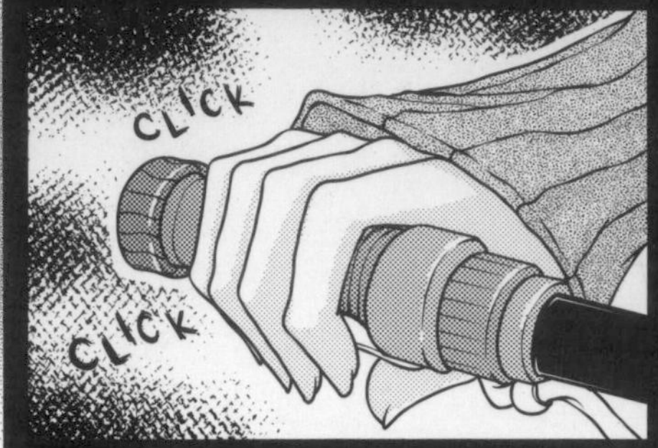

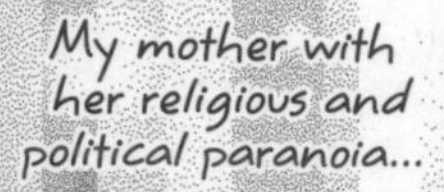

My mother with her religious and political paranoia...

SKID
And then Sarai...

What's going on with you, sis?

RAILROAD CROSSING
SKREEEEE
But why would someone want to talk to me about whether or not my sister's gay?
Unless...

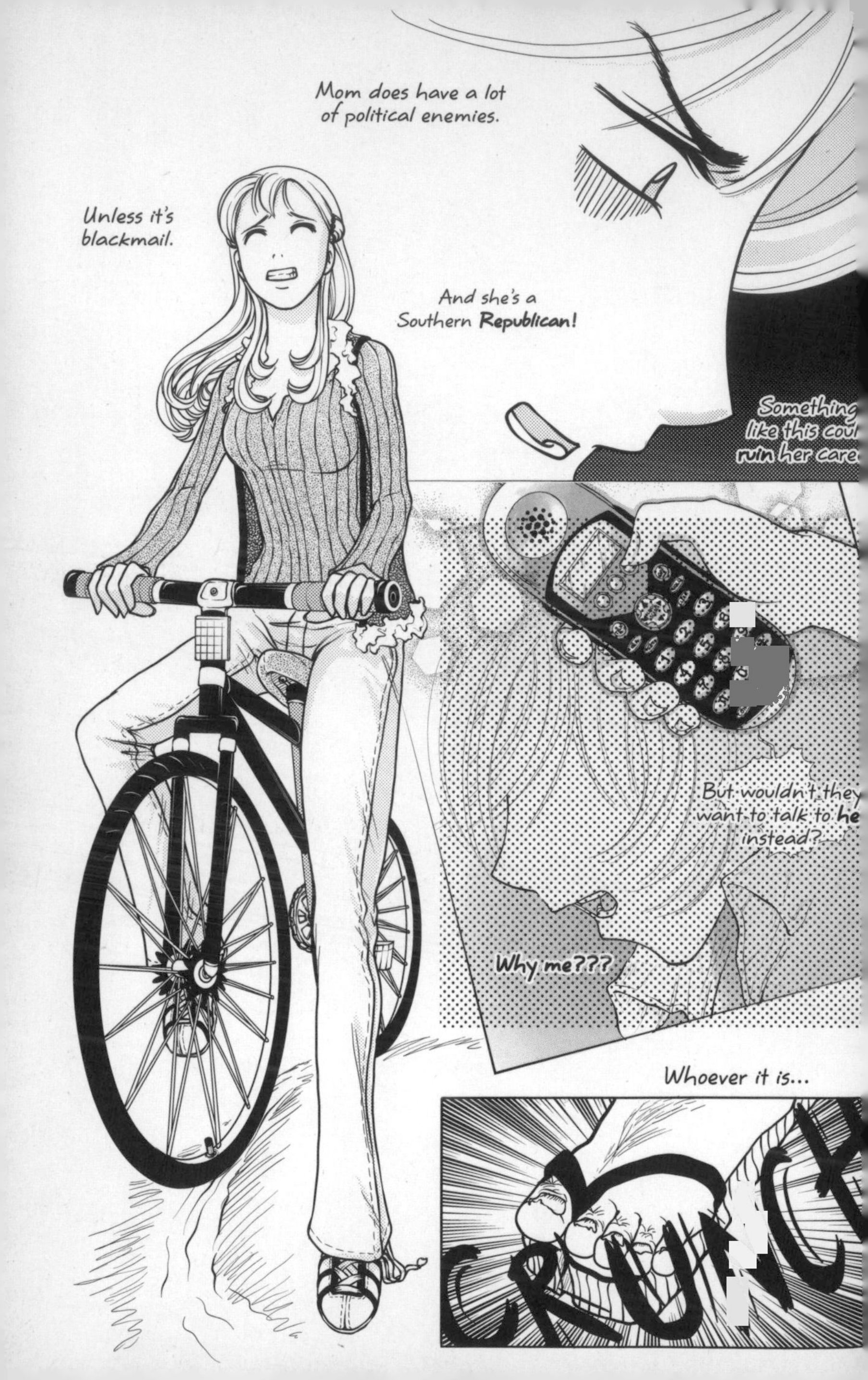

Mom does have a lot of political enemies.
And she's a Southern **Republican**!
Something like this coul ruin her care
Unless it's blackmail.
But wouldn't they want to talk to **he** instead?
Why me???
Whoever it is...
CRUNCH

I better be careful...
HEY THER PERTY LADY.
BEEN WAITIN' FOR SOMEBODY TO COME ALONG.
GOT ANY SPARE CHANGE FOR A POOR MUSICIAN DOWN ON HIS LUCK?

I TAKE CASH, CHECK, AND CREDIT.
MISA OR VASTERCARD.
JEWELRY AND VALUABLES SUBJECT TO A 5% GIFT TAX.
NO BABIES THOUGH, PLEASE
I ONLY LIKE 'EM WITH SALT AND PEPPER.
I-- I DON'T HAVE ANYTHING FOR YOU!
I'M JUST WAITING FOR SOMEBODY!
THEY SHOULD SHOW UP ANY MINUTE NOW!
HMM...
I DON'T KNOW ABOUT MEETIN' NOBODY...
BUT IF IT'S A SHOWIN 'YER EXPECTIN'
THUNK

A "showing"!?
Oh my god!!!
He's a FLASHER!!!
I GOTS A LADY!
A PERTY LADY!
A LADY NAMED BRAAAAAAAAAAAAAANDY!
BRANDY WINE!
MY PERTY LADY!
TAKES MY HOPS AND MAKES MY SPIRITS SHINE!
MY BRANDY WINE!

He's...
...He's terrible.
And this certainly isn't the guy who called me.
This is just some homeless musician looking for an audience.
That doesn't change the fact I don't have any change.
AND NOT A BLUSH LEFT
OF MY BRANDY WINE!
WOW! AWESOME!
JUST LIKE WILLIE NELSON OR STEVIE RAY VAUGHN!
I PREFER LYLE LOVETT MYSELF, BUT THANKEE!

GLAD YOU TOOK A REAL SHININ' TO MY SONG MISSEE.
NOW PAY UP.
I'M REALLY SORRY. I WASN'T LYING WHEN I SAID I DON'T HAVE ANY CHANGE.
NOT EVEN A PENNY. ISN'T THERE ANYBODY ELSE YOU COULD ASK?
WHAT'YA' MEAN "NO CHANGE"
EVERYBODY'S GOT CHANGE!

AND POOR EARL COULD USE A LITTLE CHANGE!
WHY YOU'SE THINK I'M OUT ON THE STREETS LIKE THIS?
IF MY MANAGER HAD'N FLED TOWN WITH ALL MY DOUGH AND SAID "I'LL PAY YOU TOMORROW," WHY I'D STILL BE IN BUSINESS!
I'D BE A STAR, I TELL YA!
I'M SORRY BUT I--
A STAR!
LIKE DEM BRITAINY AND AGWEEMALARIA GIRLS!
GRASP
HEY! WHAT ARE YOU DOING?!
LET GO OF MY BIKE!!!

PAY ME!!!

SCREEEEEEEEEEE

HEY!!!
HEY!!!
HANG IN THERE!
YOU'RE GOING TO BE OKAY!

*SNIFFLE
OLD MAN (HIDING)
I JUST WANTED SOME CHANGE...

LATE!
WHERE THE HECK IS SHE?
tap *tap*
Did my watch break?

KATCHA
KATC

G.D

ROLL ROLL
BUMP!

WHO...?
...ARE YOU?
HE SPEAKS?!
WHY--
AIEEEEEE
--IS THERE A GUY IN MY BED?!
WHA--?
THIS ISN'T MY BED...

LET ME GUESS.
THIS ISN'T MY ROOM EITHER, IS IT?
Okay...
...There has to be a rational explanation for this.
I just have to think. And remember why I'm in bed with a naked guy...
At least I'm still clothed.
Think, dammit!

FLICK
ON
OFF
HEY!
ARE YOU OKAY?!

END BEAT 3

BEAT 4

Okay...
Don't panic.
I'm sure there's a perfectly reasonable explanation for a girl being on my floor.

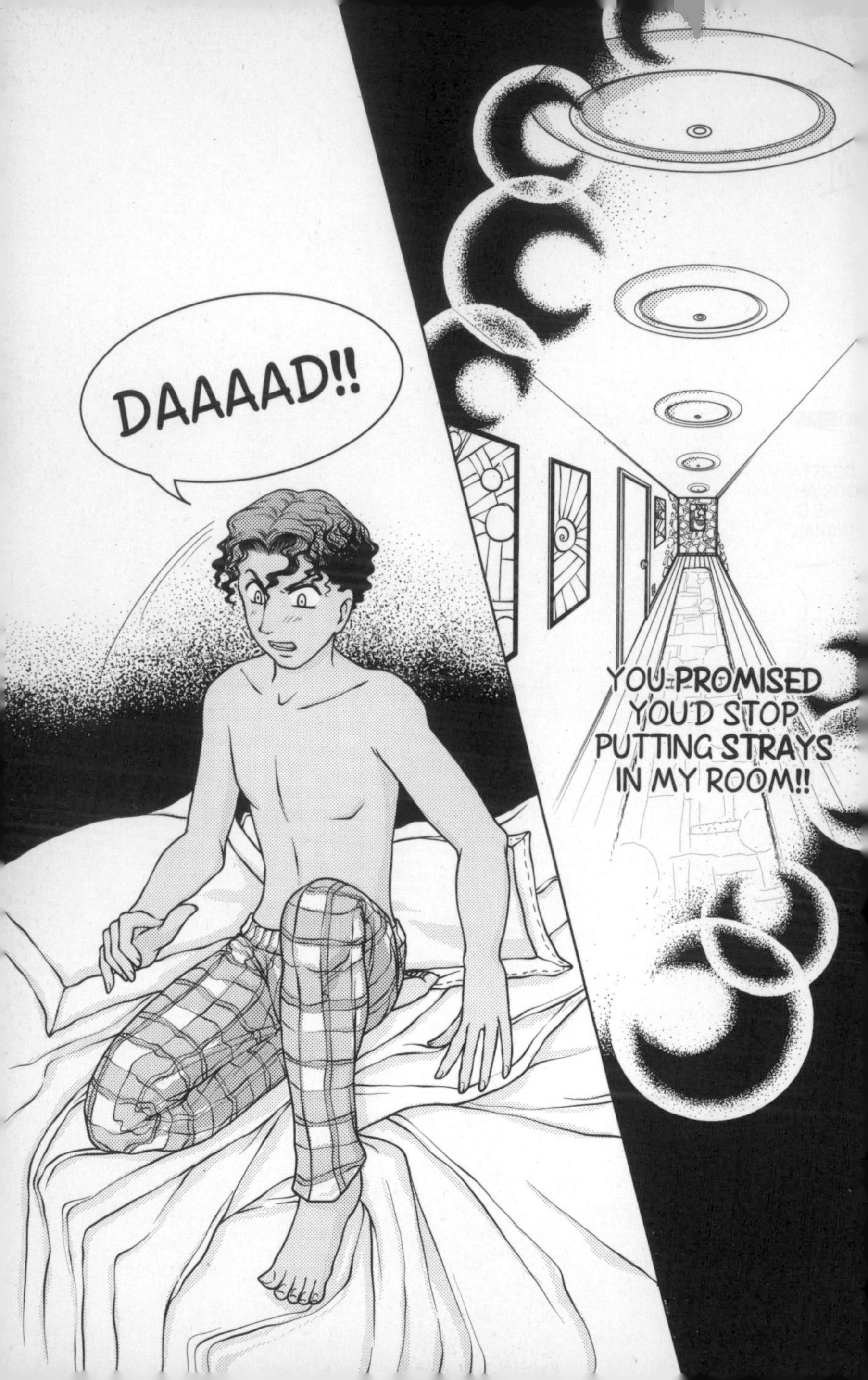
DAAAAD!!
YOU PROMISED YOU'D STOP PUTTING STRAYS IN MY ROOM!!

YOU!
STAY!!!
...I CAN DERSTAND THE STRAY OGS AND CATS, EVEN THE OCCASIONAL PARAKEET, BUT...
...A GIRL?!
...WE ARE NOT A WAYHOUSE FOR PEOPLE OR PETS!
ELIJAH!
SLAM
ELIJAH!
IS SHE AWAKE?

YOU *ARE* AWAKE!!!
AND MY! AREN'T YOU ADORABLE!
YOU POOR DARLING!
LIKE A BAB SHATSU OR SCHNAUZE
I WOULD HAVE WOKEN YOU EARLIER, BUT YOU WERE SO DARNED CUTE SLEEPING AWAY LIKE THAT!
I'M SO SORRY THAT OUR DEAR ELIJAH WOKE YOU WITH ALL THAT YELLING NONSENSE.
COME HERE, GIRL. I WON'T HURT YOU.
WHY IS HE TREATING YOU LIKE A PUPPY?
MY NAME'S PAUL!
YOU'RE SUCH A TINY LITTLE THING!
IT'S NO WONDER YOU SLEPT SO LONG!
DOESN'T ANYONE FEED YOU?

TRIP
CAREFUL!
OU BUMPED OUR HEAD ETTY GOOD GAINST THE OAD WHEN YOU FELL.
YOU ALSO TWISTED YOUR FOOT.
YOU'RE LUCKY NOTHING'S BROKEN!
I WAS SO AFRAID I'D HIT YOU WITH MY CAR WHEN YOU FELL OUT ONTO THE ROAD LIKE THAT.

YOU POOR THING!
YOU MUST BE RUNNING AWAY FROM HOME.
AT LEAST I HIT YOUR BIKE AT THE PARK, AND NOT YOU.
IT WAS DEMOLISHED!
BUT BIKES AND CARS CAN BE FIXED.
THAT'S JUS LIKE PEOPLE DUMP UNWAN PETS ON TH SIDE OF THE RO
DON'T THEY REALIZE THER ARE COUGARS AND COYOTES OUT AT NIGHT
The park!
I was supposed to meet that guy at the park, and I've missed him!
What'll I do if he doesn't call back?
HEY YOU...
...MISS PUPPY.

WHAT'S YOUR NAME?
...
IT'S LEAH.
WE'LL REPLACE YOUR BIKE. IT'S NO BIG DEAL.
BUT MORE IMPORTANT, WHAT DID THE HOSPITAL HAVE TO SAY ABOUT YOUR HEAD?
OH! SHE'D PASSED OUT, SO I THOUGHT IT'D BE EASIER TO BRING HER HOME INSTEAD.
YOU KNOW I'VE TAKEN CARE OF PLENTY OF STRAYS.
WHAT?!
SHE'S NOT SOMEBODY'S LOST PET, PAUL!
A MILD CONCUSSION AND YOU THINK BANDAGING HER FOOT AND PUTTING HER TO BED WILL HELP?!
I'M TAKING HER TO A PEOPLE DOCTOR!

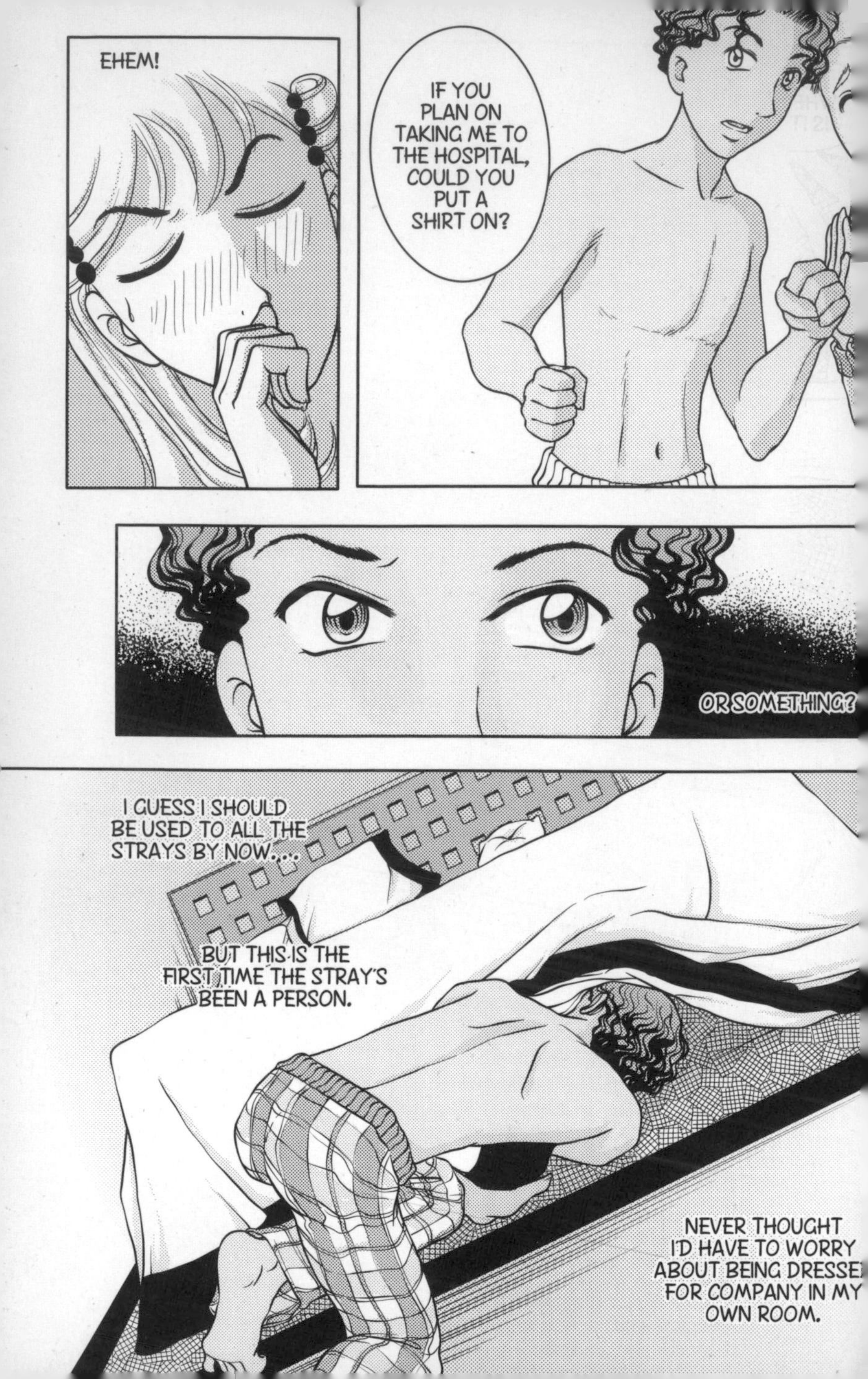
EHEM!
IF YOU PLAN ON TAKING ME TO THE HOSPITAL, COULD YOU PUT A SHIRT ON?
OR SOMETHING?
I GUESS I SHOULD BE USED TO ALL THE STRAYS BY NOW...
BUT THIS IS THE FIRST TIME THE STRAY'S BEEN A PERSON.
NEVER THOUGHT I'D HAVE TO WORRY ABOUT BEING DRESSE
FOR COMPANY IN MY OWN ROOM.

NOW WHERE IS IT?
ELIJAH!
WHY DO YOU PERSIST IN KEEPING YOUR CLOTHES UNDER THE BED?!
THERE'S ANOTHER PLACE TO KEEP THEM?

MY SHIRTS ARE NOT YOUR ANIMALS' CHEW TOYS.
CAN'T YOU KEEP THEM OUT OF MY THINGS?
YOU SHOULDN'T BE SO PREJUDICED, ELIJAH.
A PUPPY CAN'T CONTROL ITS CHEWING INSTINCT.
IT'S GENETIC.
GIRLS IN MY BED, PUPPIES CHEWING ON MY CLOTHES . . .
I'M GOING TO THE HOSPITAL, BUT . . .
. . . IF I FIND A SINGLE CAT IN MY DRESSER, OR A PARAKEET ON MY PILLOW...
I'M GETTING A LOCK FOR MY DOOR!
COMPRENDE?!

THAT'S NOT MY POINT!
THEY WOULDN'T CHEW ON MY THINGS IF YOU'D JUST KEEP 'EM OUT OF MY ROOM!
Hooooo boy . . .
I've been abducted by aliens.
And I'm definitely not in Kansas anymore!
And what's up with this family?
I can't tell if they love or hate each other.
I thought mine was the only dysfunctional family around.
. . .
. . . I hope Mom isn't home yet. She'll freak that I'm out so late.
If she realizes that I was gone because of Sarai, she's gonna ask why.

At least this is more entertaining than doing homework all night.
Though I can't believe I ruined Sarai's bike.
She's gonna kill me!
THERE, THERE GIRL.
PAT PAT
DON'T LOOK SO GLUM.
ELIJAH WILL TAKE GOOD CARE OF YOU.
I HOPE YOU WEREN'T SCARED BY ALL OF THIS COMMOTION.
WE'RE REALLY VERY NICE PEOPLE.
And I wish he'd stop treating me like a puppy.

TA-TAH NOW!
OH, MY...
IS HE ALWAYS...
OH YEAH.
YOU'VE NEVER MET A GAYER MAN.
...
WHAT'D YOU JUST SAY...?
'HAPPY' JUST DOESN'T DO HIM JUSTICE.
*USA
HEY, I'M REALLY SORRY ABOUT ALL THIS.
I'M SURE HE WAS JUST TRYING TO BE HELPFUL, BUT MY STEP-DAD CAN BE A LITTLE SHORT-SIGHTED.
HE'S REALLY A NICE GUY.
I CAN BE, TOO...
IT'S ALL GOOD.
I THINK.
HEY.
BY THE WAY . . .

I'LL CARRY YOU OUT TO THE CAR.
A HEAD INJURY CAN BE RATHER SERIOUS, AND YOU'VE BEEN LOOKING PALE.
I'D PREFER YOU DIDN'T EXERT YOURSELF...
OKAY?
NO! NO! THAT'S QUITE ALL RIGHT!
I DON'T THINK I HIT MY HEAD THAT HARD.
HMM...
YOU DON'T SAY...

BUT REALLY . . .
...YOU COULDN'T HAVE THOUGHT I'D LET YOU SAY "NO," DID YOU?
SILLY GIRL...
...YOU CAN HARDLY EVEN WALK WITH YOUR FOOT LIKE THAT.

STOP ACTING SO FAMILIAR!
CALL ME "SILLY GIRL" ONE MORE TIME, BUDDY...
...AND I'LL KICK YOU WHERE IT HURTS!
WHAT WAS THAT FOR?!
I'M TRYING TO BE NICE!
BRING IT ON! I KNOW KUNG FU!
AND I KNOW BOXING AND WRESTLING, SO DON'T EVEN START!
YOU CAN THANK MY MOTHER LATER.
IF YOU'LL JUST LEND ME A PAIR OF SOCKS, I'LL BE ON MY WAY, THANK YOU VERY MUC
YOU SIMPLY CAN'T WIN
STOP!
BZZZT!

...
I DON'T HAVE ANY SOCKS.
YOU'VE GOTTA BE KIDDING ME.
NOPE. THEY'RE ALL UNDER THE BED.
BUT THAT'S WHERE I KEEP ALL MY DIRTY CLOTHES.
THEN LEND ME THOSE.
GUYS MUST BE REALLY DISGUSTING.
WELL...
...IT'S JUST US GUYS.
LAUNDRY USUALLY SEEMS TO BE OUR LAST PRIORITY.
NO MOTHER...?

SHE LIVES IN NEW YORK.
THAT'S WHERE I'M FROM, TOO.
OR AT LEAST...
...UP UNTIL A FEW MONTHS AGO.
BUT THAT'S ANOTHER STORY...
PAUL KEEPS THE PLACE PRETTY CLEAN.
AND IN A PLACE LIKE THIS, THAT'S A REAL CHORE!
SO I DON'T THINK I HAVE A RIGHT TO COMPLAIN ABOUT THE LAUNDRY.
PLUS, HE COOKS.
REX-POO
SOLOW
SHEBA
TINY
HOW CAN I COMPLAIN ABOUT THAT?
WHY SO MANY ANIMALS, THEN?

MY STEP-DAD'S A WELL KNOWN VETERINARIAN, IF A LITTLE ECCENTRIC.
HE LETS SOME OF HIS WEALTHIER PATIENTS LEAVE THEIR PETS HERE WHEN THEY GO ON BUSINESS TRIPS OR VACATION.
HE PICKS UP A LOT OF STRAYS AND TRIES TO FIND HOMES FOR THEM, TOO.
HE FEELS SORRY FOR JUST ABOUT ANYTHING LOST AND WANDERING.
FLICKER

VRROOooooM
YOU REALLY ARE CUTE.
(IN A SORT OF INCORRIGIBLE WAY.)
I CAN SEE WHY PAUL WANTED TO KEEP YOU.
IF YOU EVER END UP IN A COMA, I'LL MAKE SURE HE PUTS YOU IN MY BED AGAIN.
IT'D BE AN IMPROVEMENT ON THE STERILE DECOR.
"CUTE"...?
DO YOU HIT ON EVERY GIRL YOUR STEPFATHER RUNS OVER?
AND I DON'T PLAN ON BEING *ANYBODY'S* DECOR.
I'M NOT HERE TO LOOK PRETTY.

I'M NOT HITTING ON YOU.
ISN'T THIS WHAT YOU GUYS CALL, "SOUTHERN HOSPITALITY?"
I THOUGHT TEXAS LOST ITS HOSPITALITY WHEN ALL YOU PEOPLE FROM CALIFORNIA AND NEW YORK MOVED HERE.
WITH THE WAY Y'ALL DRIVE, IT'D PUT ANYBODY IN A BAD MOOD!
HEH.
IT'S A LITTLE PREJUDICED DOWN HERE, TOO, ISN'T IT?
I WOULD HAVE SAID "NO, IT ISN'T" A FEW DAYS AGO, BUT...
...I GUESS PEOPLE WHO ARE DIFFERENT DO KINDA STICK OUT IN THE SOUTH...
!
HEY!
YOU GO TO THE PRIVATE SCHOOL RIGHT UP THE STREET FROM WHERE I LIVE!

HEY.
SOMETHING LIKE THAT...
. . . ARE YOU REALLY ALL RIGHT?
I MEAN. . . IT'S NONE OF MY BUSINESS, BUT...
...YOU SAID YOU WERE MEETING SOMEBODY? THEY DIDN'T DO ANYTHING TO YOU, DID THEY?
I CAN TAKE YOU TO THE POLICE STATION AFTER THE HOSPITAL, IF YOU'D LIKE.
"WHAT DO YOU MEAN?"

OH...
THANKS, BUT I'M FINE.
...I THINK IT WAS A MISUNDER-STANDING...
THE KINDA STUFF YOU MAY BE USED TO UP NORTH JUST DOESN'T HAPPEN HERE.
RRRRRRRRRR
I...

I think this all is.
I'm making assumptions and jumping to conclusions without any real facts.
But...
If it weren't for Mom, would I even care?
SO...
...YOU HAVE A BOYFRIEND?
....
HEY! WHERE ARE YOU GOING?! DON'T GET OUT YET!

SWOOSH
HOSPITAL
YOU SHOULD HAVE SEEN THE LOOK ON HER FACE!
I THOUGHT SHE WAS GOING TO FAINT!
SHE WAS LAUGHING, TOO!
WHAT'D YOUR MOTHER-IN-LAW SAY ABOUT IT?
PUT ME DOWN!
NO WAY!
IT'S MORE FUN TO ANNOY YOU.
AND WITH THAT SQUIRMING, YOU'LL JUST HURT YOURSELF IF I DO.
PUT ME DOWN!
PUT ME DOWN!
PUT ME DOWN!
PUT ME DOWN!
PUT ME DOWN!
PUT ME DOWN!

NO WAY!
YOU CALL THIS 'GENTLEMANLY?!'
AH, YOUNG ROMANCE!
IT'S SO RARE THESE DAYS TO SEE SUCH A FINE GENTLEMAN.
A 'GENTLEMAN' WOULD PUT ME DOWN AND LET ME WALK MYSELF!
MY HUSBAND WOULD NEVER HELP ME LIKE THAT!
WHEN I WAS PREGNANT, HE TOLD ME TO DRIVE MYSELF TO THE DOCTOR'S OFFICE!
HE'S NO GENTLEMAN!
THERE'S NO SUCH THING AS GENTLEMEN ANYMORE!
I GUESS REAL LADIES ARE EVEN MORE RARE!
SCARY!
WHAT LADIES?
AND I'M NOT PREGNANT! HE'S NOT EVEN MY BOYFRIEND!
GET OVER HERE AND FIGHT!

GOOD LORD, GIRL!
I DON'T THINK YOU REALIZE HOW SERIOUS A HEAD INJURY CAN GET.
IF YOU OVEREXERT YOURSELF...
...IT CAN CAUSE SWELLING AND MAKE YOU PASS OUT AGAIN.
YOU COULD EVEN DIE!
WHY DIDN'T YOU JUST SAY THAT BEFORE?
DO I LOOK LIKE THE KIND OF GUY WHO WANTS TO SCARE YOU?
YES?
ELIJAH!
WHAT ARE YOU DOING TO THIS POOR GIRL?

I THOUGHT I TOLD YOU TO STOP LECTURING THE PATIENTS!
DAD!
Dad?
But I thought...
What about...?
Doesn't his mother...?
AM I MISSING SOMETHING, HERE?

PAUL NEARLY RAN OVER THIS GIRL AND TRIED TAKING CARE OF HER HIMSELF.

HE NEVER COULD ABANDON A STRAY, COULD HE?

HOW'D YOU THINK HE FOUND ME AFTER YOUR MOTHER KICKED ME OUT?

I suppose some people divorce twice.

And...

...This guy looks kinda familiar.

But why is he living with his stepfather if his real dad also lives in town?

I wonder if he's worked with my mom before?

I could swear I've seen both of these guys in my mom's office at the Capitol.

I'M GONNA ASK YOU A FEW QUESTIONS.
PAUL'S A GOOD VET, SO I DOUBT YOUR HEAD INJURY WAS ANYTHING SERIOUS.
BUT I WANT TO DOUBLE CHECK, OKAY?
OH...
...OKAY.
CAN YOU TELL ME YOUR NAME?
LEAH REBECCA WINTERS.
HOW OLD ARE YOU, MS. WINTERS?
SIXTEEN, ALMOST SEVENTEEN.
CAN YOU TELL ME EVERYTHING YOU REMEMBER RIGHT BEFORE THE ACCIDENT?
WELL, IT STARTED WHEN I WAS BEING HARASSED BY A HOMELESS GUY AT ZILKER PARK...

"WINTERS?"
I GUESS THAT'S A PRETTY COMMON LAST NAME, BUT...
She couldn't be related to that "Winters" could she?
...Leah Winters?
If so, what was she doing alone, in a park...
...at night?

SHI-NEEEEE!
HAI-YA!
END BEAT 4

BEAT 5

YOU SURE THAT YOU'RE GOING TO BE ALL RIGHT?
DAD ALREADY GAVE YOU ENOUGH INSTRUCTIONS...
BUT IF YOU NEED ANYTHING...
...OR YOUR HEAD STARTS TO HURT AGAIN...
CALL ME!

IT'S ONLY A WEEK UNTIL MY FOLLOW-UP, RIGHT?
I'LL BE FINE.
BUT THANKS FOR BEING CONCERNED.
NO PROBLEM!
COULD YOU NOT WORRY ABOUT THE BIKE, THOUGH?
I DON'T WANT MY MOM TO FIND OUT I WAS GONE.
SO I CAN TAKE CARE OF IT.

JUST STOP GOING TO THE PARK AT NIGHT, OKAY?
AND I WON'T TELL!
I DON'T KNOW...
YOU NEVER KNOW WHO YOU MIGHT ACCIDENTALLY RUN INTO!
WASN'T HIM ON THE PHONE EARLIER.
I'M SURE OF IT.

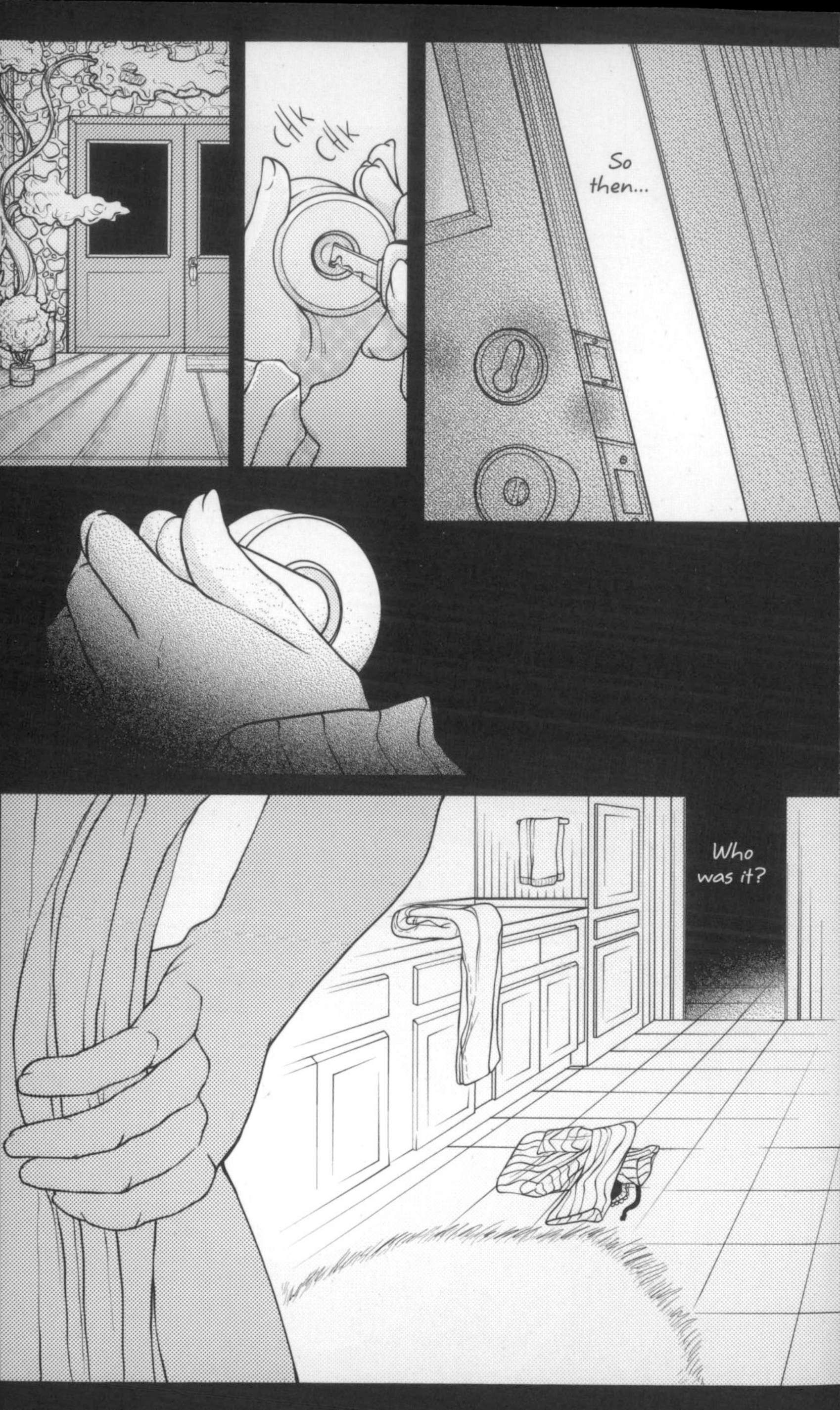
CHK
CHK
So then...
Who was it?

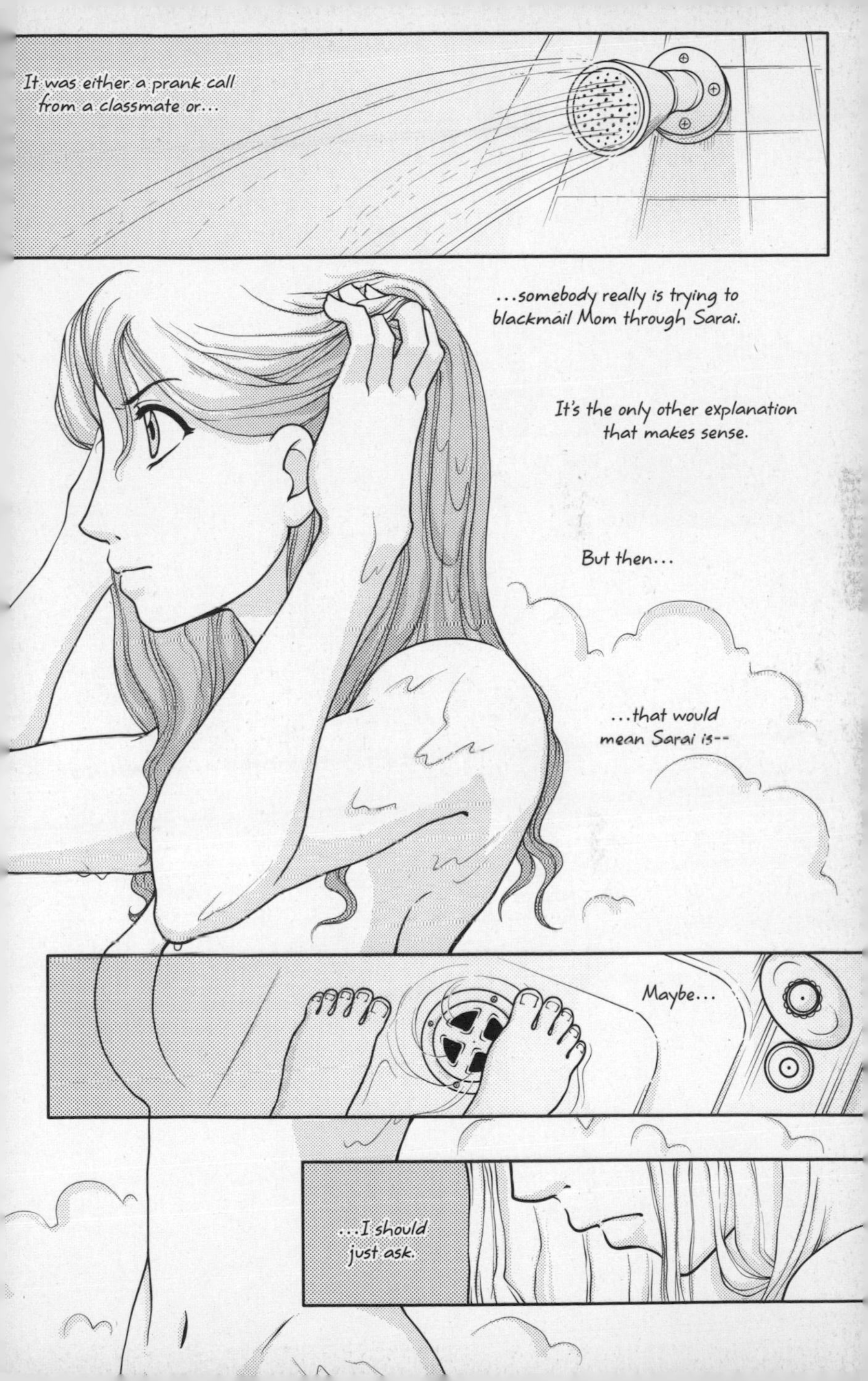
It was either a prank call from a classmate or...
...somebody really is trying to blackmail Mom through Sarai.
It's the only other explanation that makes sense.
But then...
...that would mean Sarai is--
Maybe...
...I should just ask.

CRASH
SHUFF SHUFF
What the...?!
A burglar?!
I forgot to turn the lights on when I got home!!!

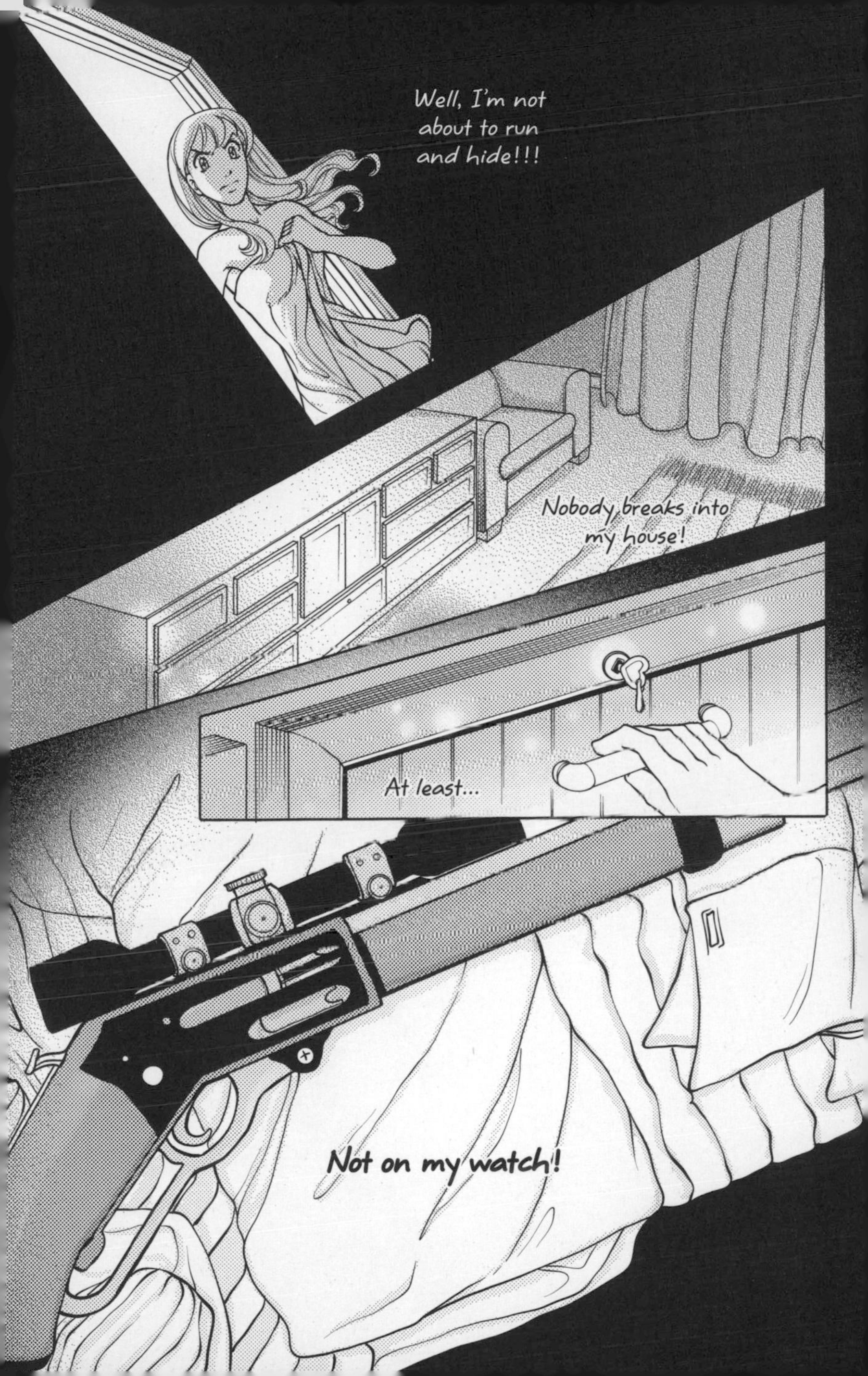
Well, I'm not about to run and hide!!!
Nobody breaks into my house!
At least...
Not on my watch!

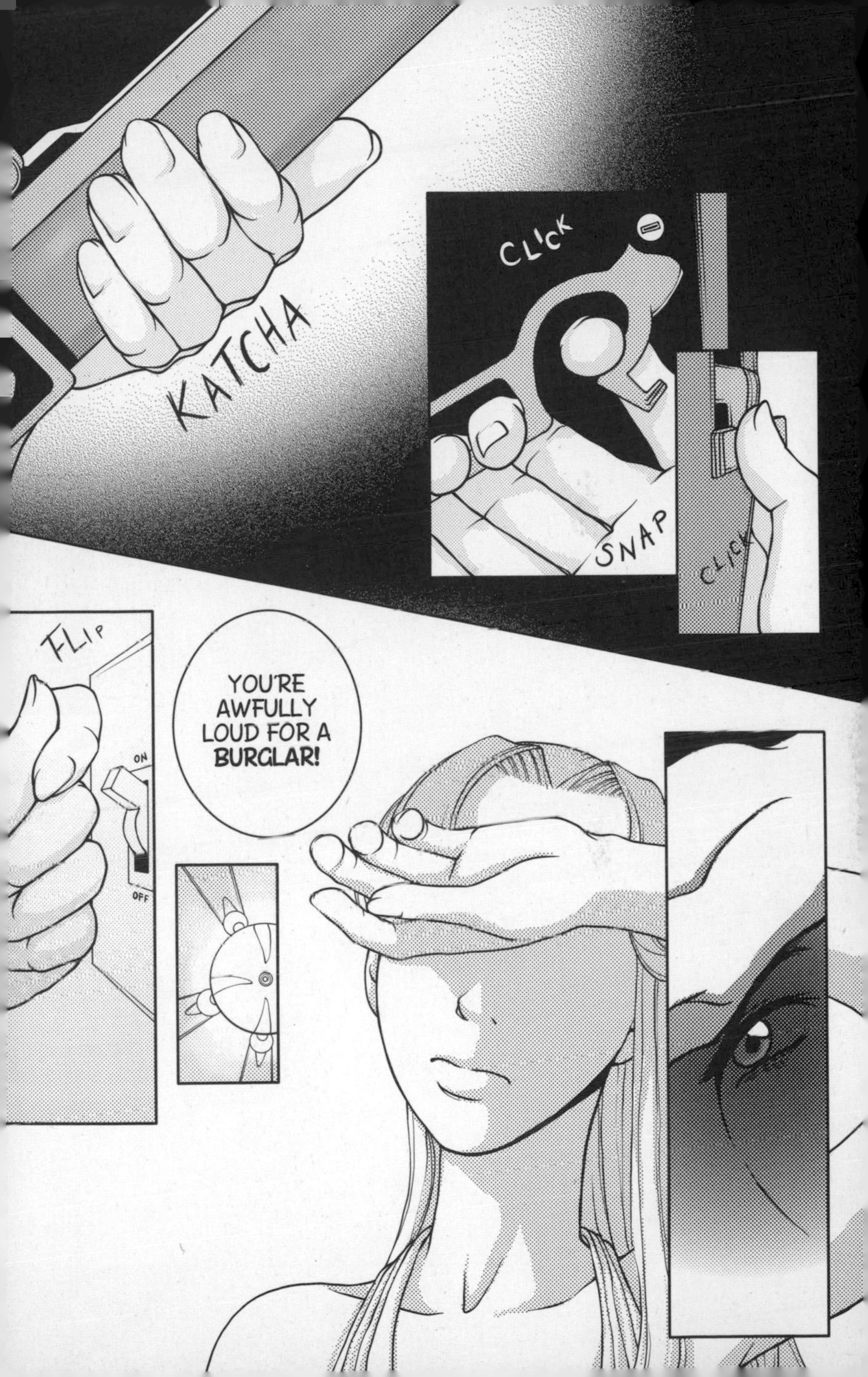
KATCHA
CLICK
SNAP
CLICK
FLIP
ON
OFF
YOU'RE AWFULLY LOUD FOR A BURGLAR!

DON'T MOVE!!!

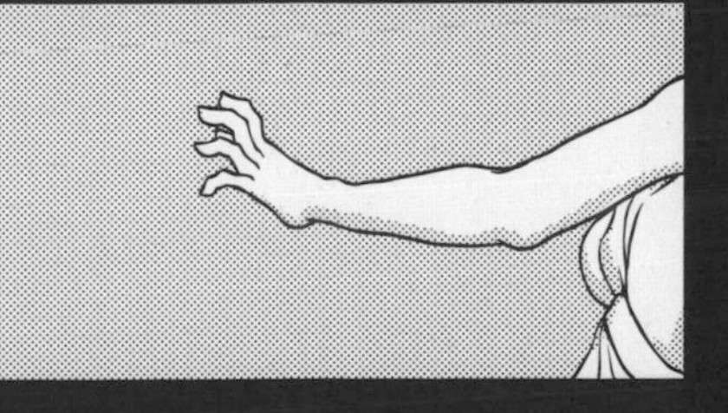

L... LEAH?!
WHY...
DO YOU HAVE...
A GUN?!
growl

WHAT THE HELL ARE YOU UP TO?!

RECRUITERS DON'T STAY OUT `TILL MIDNIGHT!
...
IT'S NONE OF YOUR BUSINESS, LEAH!
LAY OFF ME!
WHAT DO YOU MEAN, NONE OF MY BUSINESS?
I'M YOUR *SISTER!*
AND THERE'S SOMETHING ELSE I'VE BEEN WANTING TO ASK YOU.

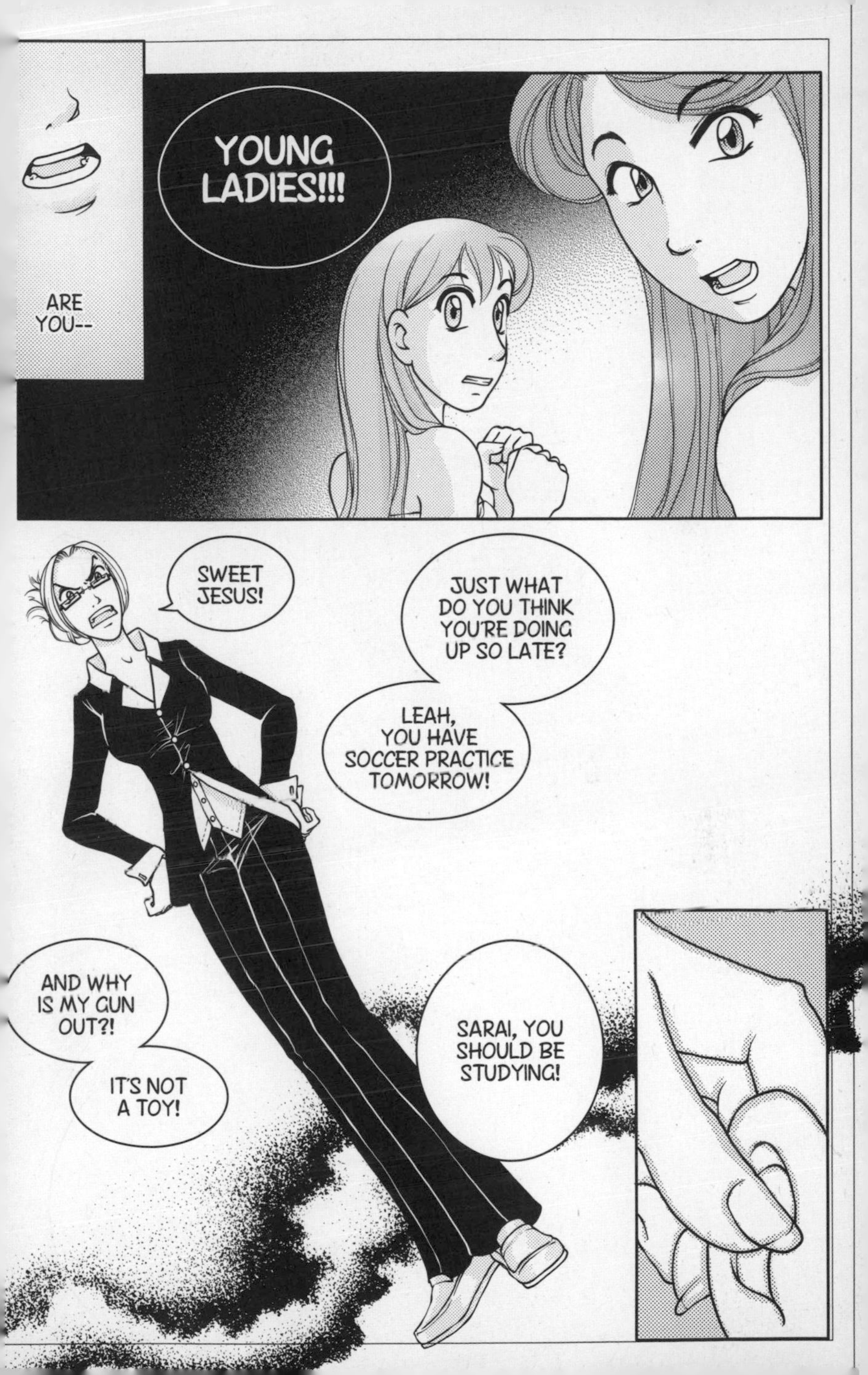
ARE YOU--
YOUNG LADIES!!!
SWEET JESUS!
JUST WHAT DO YOU THINK YOU'RE DOING UP SO LATE?
LEAH, YOU HAVE SOCCER PRACTICE TOMORROW!
SARAI, YOU SHOULD BE STUDYING!
AND WHY IS MY GUN OUT?!
IT'S NOT A TOY!

I'VE HAD ENOUGH NONSENSE FOR ONE NIGHT!
GO TO BED!
RIGHT NOW!
IF I HEAR A PEEP FROM EITHER OF YOU, IT'S EXTRA CHORES FOR THE WEEK.

YOU'RE LUCKY I'M IN A GOOD MOOD.
BAH!
GIRLS THESE DAYS!
WHAT EVER HAPPENED TO BEING IN BED BY EIGHT?
TAP TAP TAP
GOODNIGHT!
AND DON'T FORGET TO SAY YOUR PRAYERS.

Praying for a new mother...
CLICK
CLICK
Is she really asleep?
Or is she tricking us?

CREAK
Badump
Badump
Good!
She's really asleep!

TAP
TAP
RRRRRREEEEEEEE
Is Sarai even awake?
SIS?

ARE YOU CRYING?
WHY...
...
IT'S NOTHING.
I ASSUME YOU HAVE SOMETHING TO DO WITH THAT.
MY BIKE...

I WON'T TELL MOM ABOUT IT IF YOU PROMISE...
...YOU WON'T TELL HER I WAS LATE.
NOT A PEEP!
BUT WHAT IF SHE FINDS OUT?
THEN WE'LL BOTH GET IN TROUBLE.
WE'RE ALREADY BOTH IN TROUBLE.
ABOUT EARLIER...

THAT QUESTION YOU WERE GOING TO ASK ME EARLIER...
WHAT WAS IT?
...
#13

DON'T WORRY ABOUT IT.
I THINK I CAN FIGURE IT OUT ON MY OWN.
CLICK
GOODNIGHT, SIS.
THAT QUESTION...
IT'S "YES."

Yes...

END BEAT 5

VOLUME 2 OF STEADY BEAT BURNS DOWN THE CLOSET WHEN FAMILY IS OUTED -- OLD ENEMIES ARE MADE INTO FRIENDS AND FRIENDS INTO ENEMIES. HOW DO YOU FIND A WAY TO KEEP YOUR FEET IN THE MIDDLE AND ACCEPT PEOPLE SOLELY FOR THE QUALITY OF THEIR CHARACTER?

sketchbook

Elijah's expressions.

"Whenever I'm falling behind a deadline, I actually make this my background desktop image! *Laughs.* So whenever I close my work programs and go to try and play online, it reminds me to get back to work. It USUALLY works . . . >_>;"

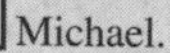

Michael.

Jessica.

"June is one of my favorite characters. She's fiery and dynamic, but she's also crazily intelligent. Girls with smarts AND style rock my world! And I have a thing for 50's style clothing with a 21st century twist. June is my styling model for *Steady Beat*. She gets to wear the COOL clothes. Look out for volume II, because you get a lot more of her there."

"What are you doing?! If you're standing in the store right now, and have just finished reading this book, go BUY IT! And then make your brother's best friend's second-cousin's sister buy it, too. ^_~ You are witness to the start of a whole new wave of American comics (or manga, if you prefer the term)! There are girls (and boys) just like you who are finally getting the stories they want and deserve. No superheroes. Not the daily funnies. REAL stories about REAL people.

"Of all the characters, Leah is probably the most l
me—when I was in high school. *Laughs.* Like Ju
she's very bright, but she hates doing the things s
doesn't want to do. Like homework, sports, or cho
(I hate homework! ;_;) But when she finds someth
she really enjoys, she pursues it full-out. I'm curi
though . . . what do you think she'll discover? Or ev
ask yourself, what's YOUR passion? Because everybo
has one . . . it just takes a little living to find it. :)"

But, if you sit and just read in the store, then how will publishers know that this is what you want to see? I'd like to keep drawing *Steady Beat*. Hopefully you'd like to keep reading it!

And maybe . . . someday . . . you'd like to draw and write your own series. You have your characters, the setting, the dilemma. You even have a title. So pay for the things you like. Put back the ones you don't. And keep on encouraging growth in the industry! And hopefully, someday, the roads we pave will help create the path to fulfill your dreams.

However, if you're comfortably at home, curled up in bed or your favorite chair . . . you deserve a cookie and a hug. :D Now go to www.rivkah.com to claim it!

"Sometimes I draw scary things. This was actually for a "Strange Machine" entry on Warren Ellis's blog—a nice distraction from the lighter tones of *Steady Beat*. The colored version can be found online at http://www.rivkah.com/illustrations/

Sarai's expressions.

This is Sarai. Elegant. Poised. Beautiful. Leah and June call her Miss Perfect. But . . . what IS perfect? And why is she this way? Is it because of their mother's expectations of her oldest daughter? Is she really just perfect, or trying to please everybody, or . . . does she try to be perfect in order to cover up something she knows her family and community would find unacceptable?

"Last week of drawing *Steady Beat*! Obviously, I was stressed."

“Did you know that *Steady Beat* was originally a webcomic? It first appeared at Wirepop.com in March 2004 It’s come a pretty long way since then! The original first chapter is still up on my website (www.rivkah.com aboutsteadybeat/) if you’d like to see how the story and art have come along since then. It amazes me how far ar can develop in the course of a single year, though . . . I look at the old chapter and I feel like someone else drew i I guess after 160 pages of drawing you learn to improve a little bit. ^_~ This book has been incredible journey bot in terms artistic expression and development of technique and style. And I look forward to continuing this journe through further volumes of both this and future series.”

Vell, here it is! The first two chapters of *Steady Beat* volume 2 are actually
lready completely penciled. I know where this story is going, girl!!!! Some-
imes I feel like it writes itself, though . . . As though it's a world that already
xists and I'm just writing the words and drawing the pictures for real people
vho aren't given life until they're on the pages and their story is told.

I hope that the characters of *Steady Beat* have as much life to them for you as they do for me, though. I really look forward to developing their character as the story progresses. Like you and me, Leah, June, Sarai, Jessica, Elijah, and Michael (you'll meet him soon enough!) grow up. They experience life, and this is their story of how they react and change.

June!

ARTON SPRING
SWIMMING POOLE SPRING
$3.50 ADULTS

"I can't believe my editor included this picture! ;_; *shame* I drew this about 3/4ths through the book when deadlines were REALLY starting to hang over my head and I was literally working 14-16 hour work days with almost NO sleep. I'd get up, work, work, work, and then go to bed and repeat the whole process again every day. No vacations. No weekends. I barely had time to EAT. ;_;

"A LETTER TO THE ASPIRING ARTIST & WRITER:
REACHING FOR YOUR DREAMS IS NEVER EASY. EVERYTHING YOU WISH TO ACHIEVE WILL BE THROUGH HARD WORK AND DEDICATION. NOTHING WILL EVER BE HANDED TO YOU. NOTHING CAN HOLD YOU BACK BUT YOURSELF.
YET, HAVING AMBITION ALSO REQUIRES A LOVE INTENSE ENOUGH TO BEAR PERSONAL SACRIFICE AND TO KEEP ON GOING, NO MATTER WHAT THE ODDS. THERE WILL BE BOTH ROUGH SPOTS AND EASY CLEAR-SAILING. EVEN WHEN YOU SEEM FAR FROM ACHIEVING ALL OF YOUR GOALS, REMAIN POSITIVE AND TELL YOURSELF YOU'LL GET THERE AS LONG AS YOU KEEP PUSHING AHEAD. SOMETIMES YOU'LL FAIL MISERABLY, BUT EVEN WHERE YOU SEEM TO FAIL, YOU WILL LEARN AND BECOME STRONGER. SOMETIMES YOU'LL FIND SUCCESS, AND IT WILL SERVE TO PUSH YOU ANOTHER STEP CLOSER TO YOUR DREAMS. THERE ARE NO ABSO-LUTES, ONLY EXPERIENCES.
WITH ENOUGH PASSION, ANYTHING IS POSSIBLE. DON'T FEAR TO BE A DREAMER OR A VISIONARY. YOU CAN DO ANYTHING. YOU JUST HAVE TO DO IT.
DON'T EVER LET GO OF YOUR DREAMS. EVEN WHEN IT SEEMS LIKE THE TIDE IS WASHING OVER YOU, STAND FIRM AND EVENTUALLY IT WILL RECEDE. LEARN FROM YOUR MISTAKES. GROW FROM YOUR TRIALS. HOLD THE LOVE AND THE PASSION FOR YOUR WORK ALWAYS IN YOUR HEART, AND YOU WILL SOMEDAY PERSEVERE."

"I've never actually been horseback riding but...someday...someday I'd really like to."

"I think the picture says it all . . . A look at how I was feeling in my personal life at the time."

Mark of The Succubus

COMING SOON

Welcome to a world that looks a lot like our own, with average kids in an average high school in an average town, that just happens to be the destination of a succubus-in-training who is on her first trip to the human world. Maeve is studying for her license to seduce and destroy, but first she needs to learn how to blend into human society. She may well be in over her pointy-eared head though, especially after one of her former teachers sets her as the focal point for a demon world coup!

Read on, because you're in for a treat, with a full chapter preview of one of TOKYOPOP's hottest new properties, Irene Flores & Ashly Raiti's Mark of the Succubus!

Barlow High
Here, the administration is **very** serious about upholding the school's impeccable reputation.
BARLOW HIGH SCHOOL
At the outset of each school year, new curricula are carefully considered…
Debated…
Implemented.

As a result, classes are both engrossing...
...and tremendously difficult.
It is a fact of which Aiden Landis remains unaware.
NOW, IF YOU'LL TURN TO ACT FIVE, WE CAN BEGIN LOOKING AT LADY MACBETH'S MOST FAMOUS SPEECH.
He daydreams his way through most of them.

AND UNLESS MR. LANDIS IS SLEEPING IN MY CLASS AGAIN, HE'LL KINDLY READ IT.
...I SEE.
MR. LANDIS!
WHAM!

WHY DON'T YOU TELL US WHY THIS SPEECH IS SO IMPORTANT?
UHHH... TH-THAT'S BECAUSE OF THE SENSE OF TRAGEDY THAT'S PERVADED THE... UHM...
RIIIIIIIIIIING!!!!
!!
LECTUREWASAMAZING GONNABELATE GOTTAGO!
WHOOOOSH

HEY, AIDEN! WAIT UP!
SHE'S GONNA KILL ME, DEV.
I BET SHE ALREADY KNOWS WHERE SHE'LL HIDE THE BODY.
YOU KIDDING? MS. MURPHEY? SHE'S GOTTA BE USED TO IT BY NOW.
ER... THANKS.
LOOK, I GOTTA RUN. I'VE GOT BOOKS OVERDUE.
AIDEN!
THERE YOU ARE.

I'VE BEEN LOOKING ALL OVER FOR YOU.
YOU DIDN'T FORGET- RIGHT, AIDEN?
BLAH BLAH BLAH BLAH BLAAHH, AIDEN.
CHU
EHEHEH. O-OF COURSE NOT.
OH, HONESTLY.
YOU SAID YOU'D TELL ME WHICH LIPSTICK MATCHED MY JACKET BETTER. I'VE GOT IT NARROWED DOWN TO THREE, BUT-
AH- SANDRA?
IS IT ALRIGHT IF WE WAIT A BIT?
I NEED TO SWING BY THE LIBRARY.
LATER THOUGH, OKAY?
NEVERMIND.

I'M REALLY SORRY!
HEY, AIDEN!
WHY ARE YOU GOING OUT WITH HER?!
MIND YOUR OWN BUSINESS, DEVIN.
IF YOU WEREN'T A MONSTROUS BITCH, I MIGHT.

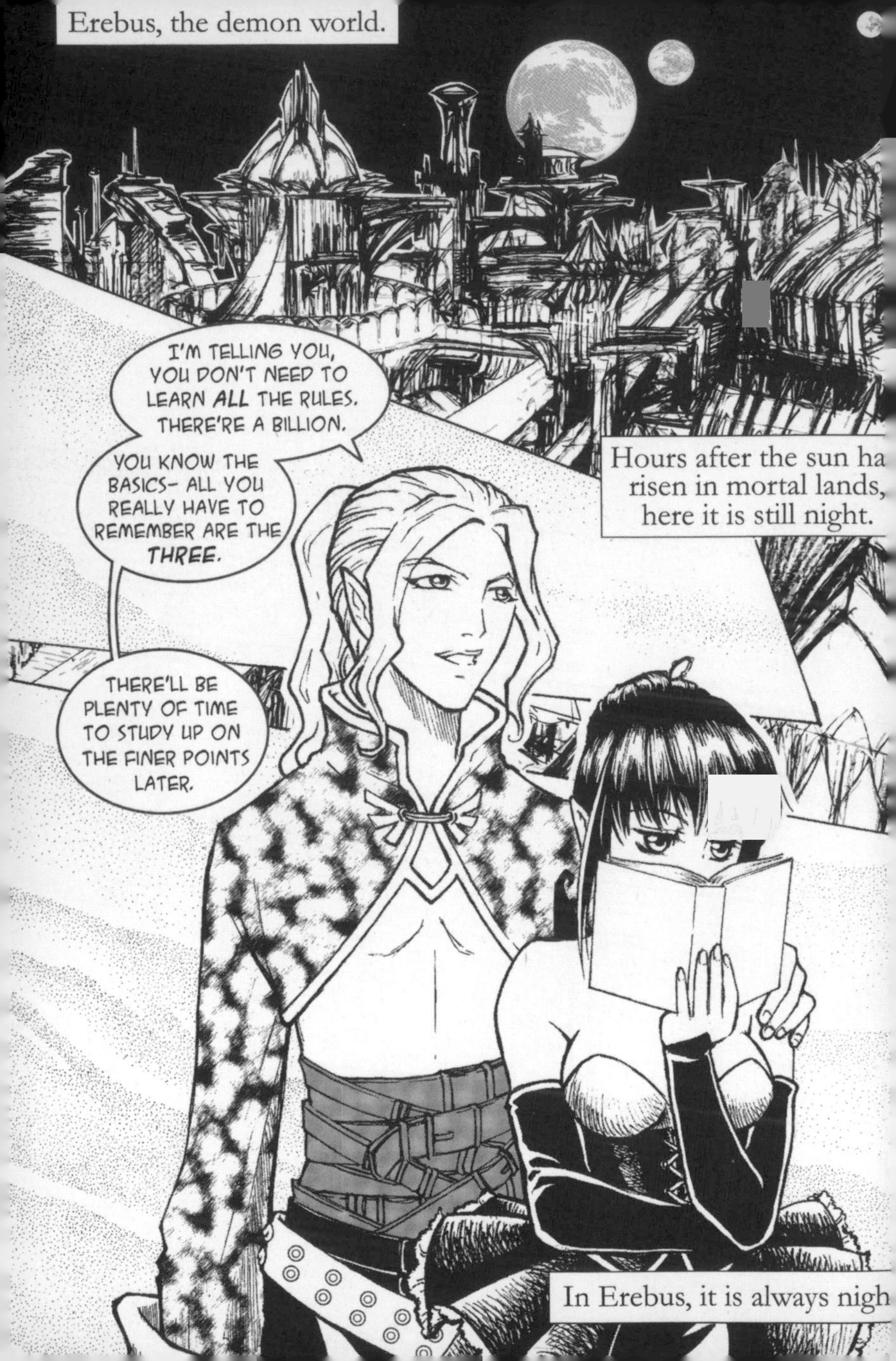

Erebus, the demon world.
I'M TELLING YOU, YOU DON'T NEED TO LEARN ALL THE RULES. THERE'RE A BILLION.
YOU KNOW THE BASICS- ALL YOU REALLY HAVE TO REMEMBER ARE THE THREE.
THERE'LL BE PLENTY OF TIME TO STUDY UP ON THE FINER POINTS LATER.
Hours after the sun ha
risen in mortal lands,
here it is still night.
In Erebus, it is always nigh

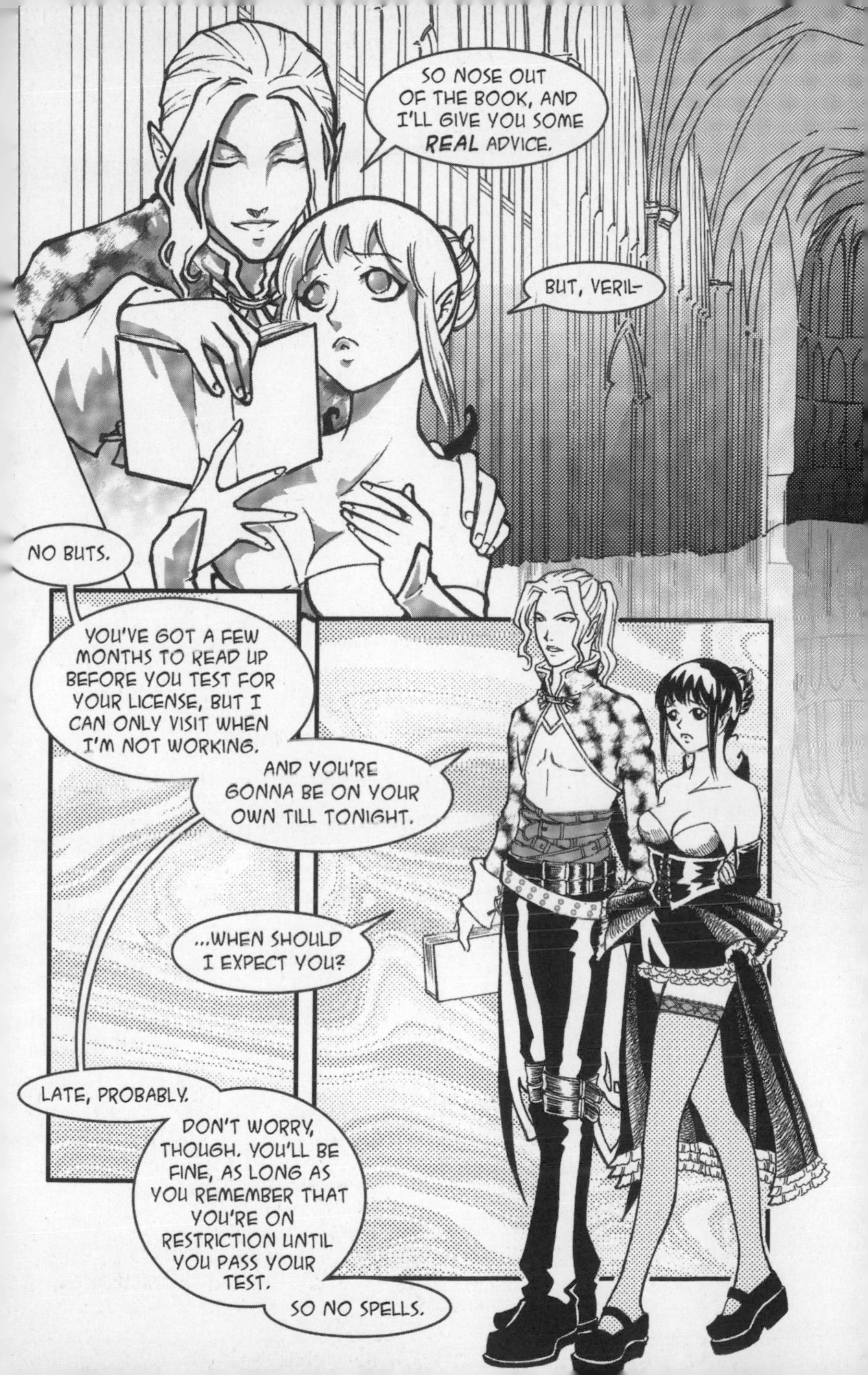
SO NOSE OUT OF THE BOOK, AND I'LL GIVE YOU SOME **REAL** ADVICE.
BUT, VERIL-
NO BUTS.
YOU'VE GOT A FEW MONTHS TO READ UP BEFORE YOU TEST FOR YOUR LICENSE, BUT I CAN ONLY VISIT WHEN I'M NOT WORKING.
AND YOU'RE GONNA BE ON YOUR OWN TILL TONIGHT.
...WHEN SHOULD I EXPECT YOU?
LATE, PROBABLY.
DON'T WORRY, THOUGH. YOU'LL BE FINE, AS LONG AS YOU REMEMBER THAT YOU'RE ON RESTRICTION UNTIL YOU PASS YOUR TEST.
SO NO SPELLS.

AND YOU DO KNOW THE IMPORTANT RULES, DON'T YOU?
UHM... LET'S SEE...
"ANY CREATURE BORN OF DAEMONKIND WHOSO SEES FIT TO WALLOW IN THE TAINT OF MORTAL MAGICKS"...
"ANY CREATURE BORN OF DAEMONKIND WHOSO MAKES REVELATIONS ONTO MORTAL SENSES REGARDING THE EXISTENCE OF OBJECTS UNNATURAL TO MORTAL UNDERSTANDING"...
AND, UHM... OH!
"ANY CREATURE BORN OF DEMONKIND WHOSO BRINGS UPON A TAINT OF FLESH AND MIND BY"...
"BY"...

HEH.
YOU DON'T NEED IT VERBATIM.
JUST 'NO HUMAN MAGIC, NO STUPID REVELATIONS, NO GETTING ATTACHED.'
"UNDER PENALTY OF THE GRAVEST VARIETY."
OR THEY KILL YOU.
RIGHT.
NOW, MOVING ALONG...
THIS IS YOURS.
IT'S A HUMAN BAG; THERE'RE SOME BOOKS.
THE MAP TO THE PLACE YOU'RE STAYING IS INSIDE, TOO.

AND NOW...
...THE FUN PART

OH!
TADAA!
THE NECKLACE HOLDS AN ILLUSION TO MAKE YOU LOOK HUMAN. THE CLOTHES ARE REAL, THOUGH; I'LL BRING MORE TONIGHT.

NOW FOR THE FINAL TOUCH.
UNTIL YOU GET YOUR LICENSE, YOU WON'T EVEN BE ABLE TO CAST A GLAMOUR, SO MAKE GOOD USE OF IT.
HERE- IT'S PERFUME. WEAR IT, AND IT'LL DRIVE ANY HUMAN YOU CHOOSE ABSOLUTELY NUTS.

AND YOU'LL VISIT TONIGHT?
OH, MAEVE. LOOK AT YOU ALREADY.
YOU'RE GONNA BE FINE.
SUCCUBI HAVE BEEN GOING TO THE HUMAN WORLD FOR CENTURIES.
BESIDES... IF ANYTHING GOES WRONG, I CAN JUST KILL THE WITNESSES AND MOP UP THE MESS.

SO RELAX!

UHM... W-WELL... SEE YOU TONIGHT, THEN.
...GOOD LUCK.

Barlow High's student library, a short time later.
THERE. BOOKS TAKEN CARE OF
NOW I JUST HAVE TO FACE SANDRA'S WRATH FOR ABOUT A WEEK.
WHAT THE..?
OH, WHAT A FABULOUS DAY THIS IS TURNING OUT TO...
BE...
THAT GIRL IS INSANE! IT'S ALMOST WINTER; SHE MUST BE FREEZING!

A MAP OF BARLOW..?
Barlow High School
UHM... EXCUSE ME...
I COULDN'T HELP BUT NOTICE... ARE YOU LOST? IF YOU'RE HAVING TROUBLE FINDING SOMEPLACE, I CAN SHOW YOU.

HUH..?
AH... YES!
HAVING JUST TRANSFERRED AND ALL.
VERY LOST VERY.
FWP
MY FIRST HUMAN... STAY CALM!
HOW DID VERIL SAY TO TRIGGER THE PERFUME..?!

SHE...
SHE'S BEAUTIFUL.
WHY'S HE STARING?

A-ALRIGHT... LET'S SEE YOUR SCHEDULE.
BIO NEXT, HUH?
I JUST CAN'T FIND IT ON THE MAP, THOUGH.

AH, WELL-
THAT'S OKAY. LOOKS LIKE WE'VE GOT A CLASS TOGETHER.
I CAN TAKE YOU THERE.
REALLY?!
THAT'S GREAT!

UHM... DON'T FORGET YOUR COAT.
IT'S COLD OUT.
...MY?
OH, YES! MY COAT!
NEED A COAT...
WHERE'S A COAT?
!!

I'VE FOUND IT!
THIS ISN'T SO HARD... HE DOESN'T EVEN SUSPECT!
THE HELL..?
AW, MAN...

The Registry building.
One of Erebus' thre
governmental center
It is a place of detailed records, and of complicated policies, and of rules.
Every demon knows the Registry building.

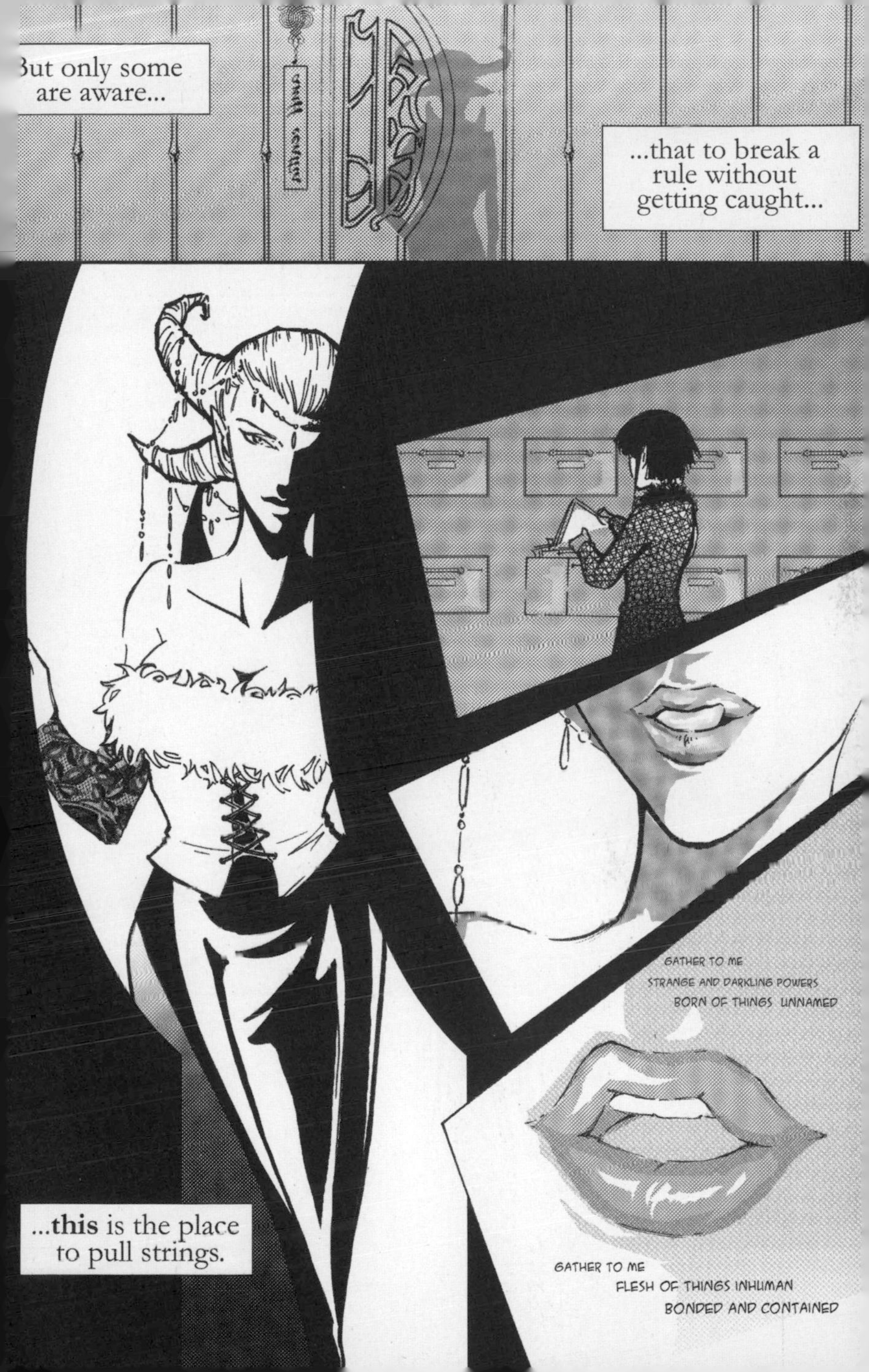
But only some are aware...
...that to break a rule without getting caught...
...**this** is the place to pull strings.
GATHER TO ME
STRANGE AND DARKLING POWERS
BORN OF THINGS UNNAMED
GATHER TO ME
FLESH OF THINGS INHUMAN
BONDED AND CONTAINED

GATHER T ME
DAEMON'S HEART AND SPIRIT
!!
AAAAAAHH!
WEAKENED...
HELPLESS...
PAINED.
...ASTONISHING.
WHOEVER WOULD HAVE IMAGINED THAT HUMANS COULD MANAGE TO CREATE A MAGIC SO POWERFUL?

NOW.
JUNAEL, ISN'T IT?
YOU'RE FAIRLY CLEVER, FOR AN IMP. I SUSPECT YOU UNDERSTAND A GOOD DEAL ABOUT THE SORT OF SPELL I'VE USED TO BIND YOU.
CONSIDER IT A PROPOSAL.
YOU RECALL MAEVE– I BELIEVE YOU HELPED HER WITH THE PAPERWORK FOR HER PERMIT.
I'D LIKE YOU TO KEEP AN EYE ON HER.

AS HER TEACHER, I SENSED A BIT OF... IMPROPRIETY ABOUT HER.
I'D LIKE YOU TO INFORM ME IF SHE DOES ANYTHING RASH.
WOULD YOU?
THEN I MUST EXPRESS MY CONDOLENCES.
YOUR STATUS AS HEAD SUCCUBUS NOTWITHSTANDING, IT IS THE RESGISTRY'S POLICY REGARDLESS THAT-
NOW, NOW...
YOU DON'T EXPECT THAT I'D REQUEST YOUR SERVICES UNREWARDED, DO YOU?

IF YOU HELP ME...
THE SPELL IS LIFTED.
AND YOU, LITTLE IMP, NEEDN'T DIE WRITHING IN AGONY.
...WHEN ALL IS SAID AND DONE...
...I SUSPECT YOU SHALL REGRET THIS.

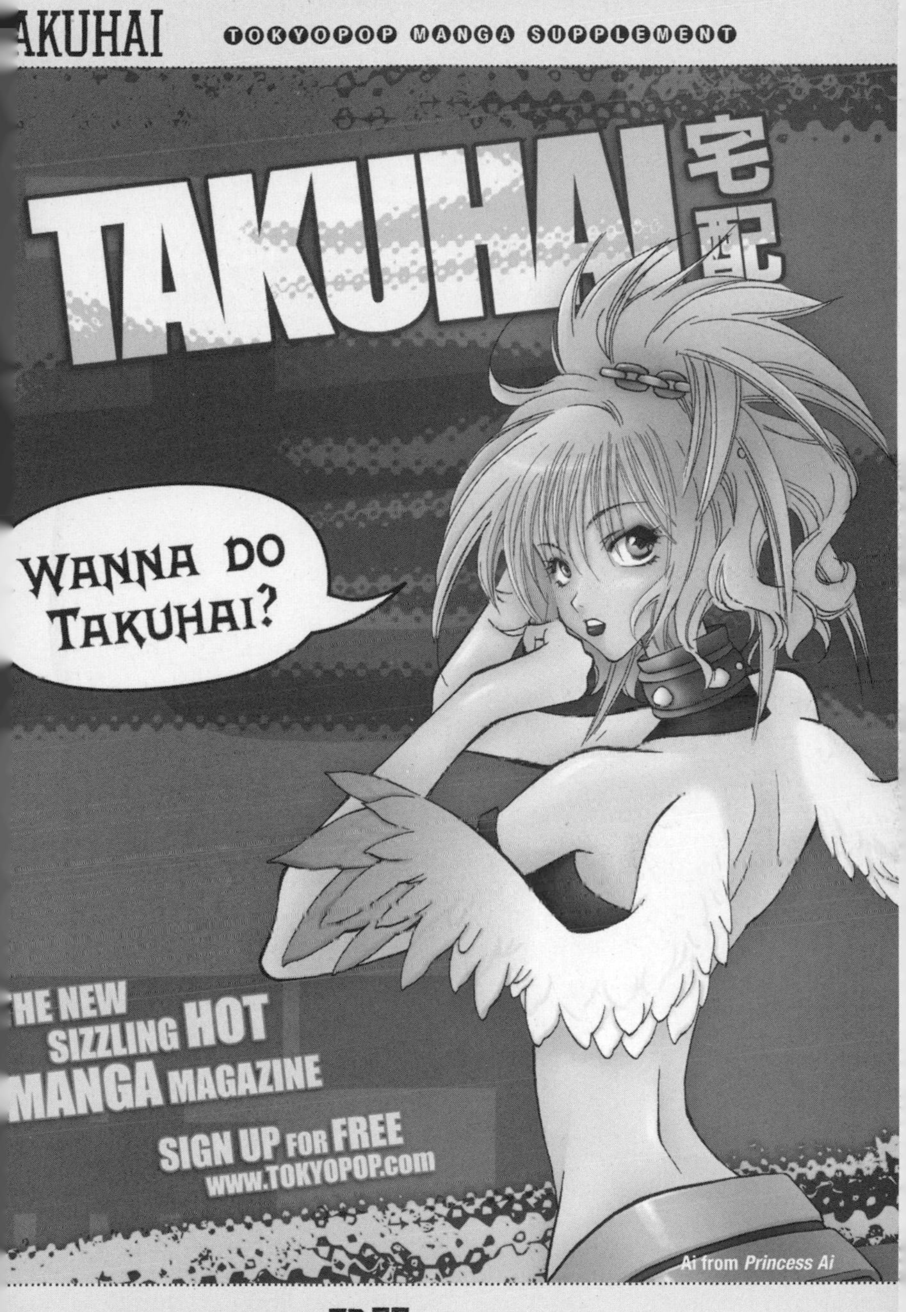
AKUHAI
TOKYOPOP MANGA SUPPLEMENT
TAKUHAI 宅配
WANNA DO TAKUHAI?
HE NEW SIZZLING HOT MANGA MAGAZINE
SIGN UP FOR FREE
www.TOKYOPOP.com
Ai from Princess Ai

WWW.TOKYOPOP.COM/SHOP
0 00000 00000 0

NO
OITERING
T
TEEN
AGE 13+

BY MASAMI TSUDA

KARE KANO

Kare Kano has a fan following for a reason: believable, well-developed characters. Of course, the art is phenomenal, ranging from sugary sweet to lightning-bolt powerful. But above all, Masami Tsuda's refreshing concept—a high school king and queen decide once and for all to be honest with each other (and more importantly, themselves)—succeeds because Tsuda-sensei allows us to know her characters as well as she does. Far from being your typical high school shojo, *Kare Kano* delves deep into the psychology of what would normally just be protagonists, antagonists and supporting cast to create a satisfying journey that is far more than the sum of its parts.

~Carol Fox, Editor

BY SHIZURU SEINO

GIRL GOT GAME

There's a fair amount of cross-dressing shojo sports manga out there (no, really), but *Girl Got Game* really sets itself apart by having an unusually charming and very funny story. The art style is light and fun, and Kyo spazzing out always cracks me up. The author throws in a lot of great plot twists, and the great side characters help to make the story just that much more special. Sadly, we're coming up on the final volume, but I give this series credit for not letting the romance drag out unnecessarily or endlessly revisiting the same dilemmas. I'm really looking forward to seeing how the series wraps up!

~Lillian M. Diaz-Przybyl, Jr. Editor